all out

IMPACT

ISBN (Paperback): 979-8-9888474-2-7

Library of Congress Control Number: 2024915077

Published By: Burnout To All Out Publishing

Cover Design By: Danielle Damrell Creative Collective, Inc.
Collaborative Book Management + Life Story Interviews By: Danielle Damrell
Editing and Contributions By: Georgia Curtis

The author disclaims responsibility for adverse effects or consequences from the misapplication or injudicious use of the information contained in this book. Mention of resources and associations does not imply an endorsement.

IN LOVING MEMORY OF

My Grandmother

*You were the example of an All Out life,
a fulfilled soul when the angels came to get you.*

*You taught me the importance of
having compassion and serving others.*

*You portrayed resilience by continually
recreating yourself when approached with
headwinds in life.*

*You demonstrated to me how to stay
connected spiritually and live with purpose.*

You are the epitome of All Out impact.

Katherine Davis Windell

MARCH 13, 1925 - JUNE 27, 2024

all out IMPACT

THE ACTIONABLE ADVICE OF 23 ENTREPRENEURS
ON A MISSION TO EMPOWER OTHERS
TO LIVE ALL-OUT, IMPACTFUL LIVES.

ADD *your* IMPACT STATEMENT
AFTER FINISHING THIS BOOK:

_____

_____

_____

_____

contents

foreword

WHY IMPACT?

Every winter, before the new year, I sit back and start to think about what my true north will be. I set an intention or key purpose for the new year. I truly believe we evolve as business owners. What drove us to get where we are today will not continue to drive and motivate us to where we're headed tomorrow. *How* you impact changes from year to year.

As business owners, our purpose and true north evolve. If we don't reassess them year after year, we start to get stale—slowing down and getting stuck—because we often lose sight of our true purpose once we achieve that first goal.

When I first escaped from the corporate world, my impact came down to doing whatever it took to prove myself as an individual and match my income as a medical doctor in big pharma. I was stuck in a loop of operating the only way I knew how—to hustle my way to success. I continuously repeated the cycle of chasing that next income goal and achieving it at whatever cost—most often, burnout.

I was micro-focused within my own little bubble of impact—only concerned about the impact I was making on myself and my family. I had put on my own oxygen mask and wasn't looking at the world around me.

My impact was all about *ME*—in other words, the little *"i."*

At the beginning of my career, this approach to impact seemed to work. I was seemingly successful at it. For the next several years, I focused on how much I could make, what kind of nest egg I could build, and how I could create a lot of income to diversify and invest in other places.

I NEEDED TO REASSESS WHERE I WAS HEADED NEXT IN ORDER TO FULFILL MY PURPOSE.

At work, I was the queen of hustle and bustle. Working long hours and drinking excessive amounts of coffee to stay alert caused havoc within my body and wrecked my nervous system's ability to function properly. From the outside, it seemed as though I was "successful," although I began to quickly feel the tension of operating out of alignment with the impact I knew I was capable of making. **I needed to reassess where I was headed next in order to fulfill my purpose.**

As I continued working in an executive-level role within the pharmaceutical industry, I attended a senior leadership training where I was challenged to write a personal mission statement. I wrote—

"I want to be the leader that sets the example that you can be happy, healthy, and wealthy, all at the same time."

This moment led to my awakening. I suddenly realized why I felt out of alignment with my purpose. I had become a corporate minion who was stagnant because I was too afraid of the unknown. At this time, all I knew was how to be "Dr. Henault"—an identity where my voice was valued and not constrained. Yes, I had generated some wealth and made a name for myself, but it was all about me and the nest egg that I could create within my small circle of influence. I had limited my own impact to be about that little *"i,"* and it was time for that to change.

This led me to discover the importance of the bigger "I," the capital "I"—*IMPACT.*

This realization happened over time, but in reflection, it was profound. I had achieved self-satisfaction, but this journey wasn't meant to be about self-rescue. I broke free, but eventually, I turned back and saw countless others trapped in their own misery. That's when I created the 'Burnout to All Out' brand. I realized I could help others wrestling with similar struggles to overcome the anxieties of changing paths and brave the uncertainties of entrepreneurship to create a life of happiness, health, and wealth. It really is possible to have all 3, but it starts with an understanding of expansive impact.

I was focused on a three-tiered approach to impact:

+ Family
+ Business (Clients and Team)
+ Community at Large

By the end of 2023, I knew I was making an impact on my family and business, but I also wanted to make an impact on humanity. I began asking myself the following questions during my solo winter planning retreat in the mountains every year.

+ *How can we create and find purpose in what we do?*

+ *How can we create success in a way that gives back to humanity?*

What I uncovered is that it goes back to generational impact.

Generational impact doesn't just affect my immediate family. My great-grandmother always used to say, "Your generational job is to make sure you leave this upcoming generation better than the last."

As I sat in the cabin, I reflected on the mountains that our ancestors had to climb. They reached certain peaks that became our baseline. Where they end, we begin. Climbing mountains takes grit, determination, and challenging the status quo. It's not easy, but it ultimately creates an elevated baseline for future generations to begin their climb. Where we end, the next generation begins.

How do we gear up for the climb?

We ask hard questions.

In All Out Impact, each author had the opportunity to answer *7 Big Questions* about impact. These questions may appear simple at first glance, but they have been specifically curated and presented in a manner that aims to maximize self-analysis.

1. How do you define impact?

2. Looking back over your life, who has impacted you most, and what specific advice or guidance from them has not only influenced your personal growth but also significantly impacted the direction of your professional career?

3. Think about the personal challenges you've overcome in your life. How did the obstacles that you've overcome play a part in the impact that you make now?

4. Reflect on a moment in your professional life that you perceived as a failure. How did this experience lead to your most significant lessons of impact? Share how you have applied these lessons to positively influence your life and the lives of others.

5. How do you ensure your business practices align with ethical and sustainable principles while balancing profitability with making a positive impact?

6. What role do partnerships and collaborations play in amplifying the impact of your business? How do you identify and cultivate meaningful relationships with other business leaders?

7. Looking ahead, what are your aspirations for the future impact of your business, and how do you plan to continue evolving and innovating in this area?

Within the pages of this book, you'll discover the stories of 23 entrepreneurs who have made the choice to elevate their impact and share the stories, lessons, and influences that have made a lasting impression on their journeys. This book is all about the big *"I."* It's about prioritizing honesty, lessons in failures, and the importance of partnerships and collaborations.

All Out Impact is a choice. It's the decision to have a strong effect on someone or something positively. This book is about impacting *YOU*, the reader, and giving you the tools and advice you need to live your most fulfilling life—an all-out life.

An all-out life is possible for you, your family, your business, and the community at large... and it all starts with the big *"I"*—**IMPACT.**

maximize your impact

SOME MUST-READ NOTES TO HELP
YOU GET THE MOST OUT OF THIS BOOK!

Included below are some housekeeping notes to follow that will help you gain the most impact from this book.

+ As you begin reading, you might notice that this book's structure is unique—not every question is answered in every chapter. Editors have refined the responses and interviews to deliver the most impactful and relevant insights tailored to you, the reader. The focus of this book is to convey the most impact-driven explanations with the most actionable takeaways.

+ All parts of a person's story are important and worth sharing, so we have recorded each author's interview and put together a complimentary podcast called the *All Out Impact Podcast* with the extended conversations! Search *"All Out Impact Podcast"* anywhere podcasts are found, or you can find

QR codes to each of their extended interviews located in the "Full Author Conversations" section toward the end of this book.

+ Each chapter begins with a brief author bio and links to their LinkedIn (LI) and website (if applicable) to interact with them and learn more about their experiences, stories, and ways they are called to impact this world.

+ Toward the back of this book, you can find the "Create-Your-Own Actionable Impact Index." This section has blank lines for YOU to create your own index based on the authors' chapters, quotes, and resources you find the most inspiring throughout this book. Use this customized index for quick and easy references whenever you reflect on the book.

+ Throughout the book, you'll discover additional resources, such as a QR code to download a free guided breathwork session and impact-focused podcast episodes, to support your journey.

+ Look out for "Life-Changing Quotes" throughout this book. The authors compiled quotes from influential figures, mentors, and others who have greatly impacted the course of their lives and businesses.

"A RISING TIDE LIFTS ALL BOATS."

John F. Kennedy

becoming the ultimate mentor

MELISSA HENAULT

in /melissa-henault

READ MORE OF MELISSA'S STORY:

burnouttoallout.co/about-melissa-henault

Melissa is a business strategist & coach and lead generation expert who elevates burned-out entrepreneurs to all-out CEOs by teaching them how to implement sustainable growth methods and modern solutions to launch and scale their businesses in the digital era.

Prior to founding her company, Burnout to All Out, Melissa was an overworked senior leader in a Fortune 500. In an effort to establish an exit plan, she took her corporate leadership skills to the Internet to build her fi rst E-commerce business. In less than two years, Melissa grew her business revenue beyond her corporate income, retired from the pharmaceutical industry at the age of 35, and cataloged her strategies for success into various offers to help other entrepreneurs.

Melissa quickly scaled her coaching business into a multi-million-dollar organization. Through her online courses, group coaching programs, and live events, Melissa trains entrepreneurs to develop their personal brands, build profitable businesses, and effectively manage their businesses in ways that support their ideal lifestyle.

Melissa is a 3x best-selling author and a featured expert on BizTV. She has been featured in leading global publications, including The New York Times, Inc., NBC, and Business Insider, and is the host of the top-rated podcast show, Burnout to All Out Podcast.

How do you define impact?

It's evolved for me through the years, but right now, impact is: "How are you creating a positive contribution to the collective?" How are you honing in on your God-given gifts in a way that creates a positive ripple effect on the rest of humanity, driving us toward the greater good? I'm now at a place where I'm constantly evaluating whether my activities and actions are positively impacting the greater good. This goes all the way down to every business decision.

In the past, previous versions of me have chosen to participate in business deals and business opportunities 100% for income, which totally backfired on me for good reason. I genuinely believe that the universe, God, Spirit, you name it, gives us feedback.

If we're getting behind something that's not with the best of intentions for humanity, you're going to get feedback on that. What are your true intentions? Are they aligned to helping others in whatever ways you're gifted? Are they to serve and to help others, or is it solely selfish? If you're pursuing something over and over again and continuing to get negative feedback, maybe you should revisit what you're pursuing.

Two or three years ago, it was a no-brainer for me to promote a "healthy" alcohol and organic wine company because I saw the bottom-line income opportunity. Even though, on paper, it made all the sense in the world to make a ton of money, I hit every roadblock known to man for 2 years until finally, I said, "Okay, universe, I get it." My dad died of alcoholism, and it runs in my family. I am good at sales and running businesses, but this was a huge risk of a negative impact on humanity by growing this business and promoting toxins and alcoholism.

Looking back over your life, who has impacted you most, and what specific advice or guidance from them has not only influenced your personal growth but also significantly impacted the direction of your professional career?

My great-grandmother was the first to tell me at a young age to "leave a better opportunity for the next generation than you had."

Some of the most incredible wisdom also comes from my mother's mother, my grandmother, who was one of the most multifaceted women of her time. She did things that were so unconventional most people wouldn't even consider them possible.

She recreated herself so many times. In her early fifties, she got a divorce after having five children and raising them all the way through college. After her divorce, she got a real estate license and became a real estate agent. It was uncommon for a woman of her generation to get a real estate license, especially considering she had spent many decades as a full-time homemaker within an affluent family due to her ex-husband's entrepreneurial success. She was able to build a real estate empire that generated recurring income that she was able to live off of until she was 99 years old.

In the 1970s, she got her pilot's license and took all 5 of her kids on a flight to Myrtle Beach by herself. To her, there were no boundaries of what you could and couldn't do. She traveled all over the world by herself all the way into her late seventies and always had the most eclectic collections of worldly things in her home.

Even though she had 5 children, she also hosted foreign exchange students. Over the holidays, when the foreign kids at the local university couldn't get home, she hosted them all in her house. She had a lot of people in her family, so she could have easily said, "There is no space," but she always made enough food and room at the table for everyone on every holiday we ever had. There were always friends or family who knew they were welcome and treated as family to anyone who didn't have one of their own. She was so loving and greeted people with open arms.

Going back to the days of segregation in the sixties, my grandparents were members of a country club. My mom had a friend who was a woman of color, and one time she asked her mom if she could bring her to the country club. My grandmother quickly replied, "Absolutely! You guys go have a good time." My mom said that when she and her friend showed up at the club, her parents were already there, sitting at a dining table. My grandparents had gotten there before them, just to make sure that the club didn't give the girls any kind of nonsense because they were bringing in someone who didn't look like the rest of them. This is just another story of how my grandmother set the example of inclusivity for my mom, who ultimately set that example for me.

Another thing my grandmother taught us was to keep our eyes open for the underdog—support them and welcome them in. She also demonstrated to us that just because you were a mother in the 1960s doesn't mean there are limitations on what you can do and who you can become. Even if you're a homemaker for the first half of your life, you can recreate yourself and build wealth in the real estate world if you want to.

The last thing that massively impacted me was her level of commitment to her spiritual practice and health. I lived with her for a period of time, and she was out in the pool swimming laps every day. She always had a one-year Bible and worked through a new one every year. She would sit with it for an hour each day, pen in hand, before she did anything else. I believe these behaviors and practices are what led her to a healthy age of 99 before departing us. She was committed to her spiritual and health practices, and she clearly held no resentment for others in her life. My grandmother was as loving and forgiving as they come, while also embodying a spirit of adventure.

Think about the personal challenges you've overcome in your life. How did the obstacles that you've overcome play a part in the impact that you make now?

Early into my entrepreneurship journey, I had this mindset of *"When I, then I'll..."* When I achieve this, I'll feel safe. When I hit this number, I'll be happy.

The reality is, as entrepreneurs, we're horizon chasers—there's always a horizon.

No matter what you achieve, if you're racing for a sense of safety or self-accomplishment, know that when you get there, you'll still feel empty if you depend on the next achievement to satisfy you. That's just how entrepreneurs are wired as horizon chasers. But that's also why I've been working a lot with my clients on rewiring how we define who we are and how we need to be satisfied and content in our current state.

We are not defined by our business.

We are not defined by the numbers.

We are not defined by a good month or a bad month.

The more you can detach yourself from self-worth as a monetary number or the size of your client or follower count, the more you will operate from a healthier space.

I want to underscore what I've learned along my journey as an entrepreneur—**we're in a spiral.**

Personal growth and spiritual ascension are not a straight shot. We spiral *upwards*. While we spiral, we revisit similar challenges that we've likely experienced in the past. The truth is, we know we're evolving and growing when we hit similar challenges but approach them differently because of the lessons we learned from previous experiences.

Over the years of growing and scaling my business, I've had many disappointments, flops, and things that went wrong. I even look back at the version of myself from just a couple of years ago, when I hit my first million dollars in revenue. If you look at photos of me from back then, I am swollen. The cortisol in my body was through the roof. I didn't have the skill set to manage the stress, and I was in a fight-or-flight mentality. I didn't have a lot of resiliency.

What I've learned through every disappointment is how to just feel it and move through it instead of trying to avoid it. One of the biggest challenges most of us face is trying to avoid disappointment and failure. In the act of trying to avoid it, we're driving ourselves crazy instead of recognizing and expecting that this is just a part of the human experience.

Just like goodness and tragedy exist in the natural world, **there are wins and losses in life.** When you look outside, as barbaric as this sounds, it's violent. Bad things happen—mass casualties, unfair job losses, rising inflation rates, and so on. This is

> ## THE REAL QUESTION IS—HOW CAN YOU MOVE *THROUGH* THE DISAPPOINTMENT?

the unfortunate part of humanity. It's not always going to be rainbows and unicorns. If we try to avoid it, we're putting ourselves in a little bubble and setting ourselves up for constant disappointment instead of accepting that we will face hard things.

The real question is—How can you move *through* the disappointment?

The key to success is resiliency. The only way to move through obstacles healthily is to build skill sets and tools to work *through* the hardship and the disappointment. Again, you need to simply allow yourself to move through it instead of avoiding it. Also, ask yourself, "What can I learn from this?"

Failure is an opportunity to learn. When I look back at every moment in my journey of entrepreneurship, even the times when I've had the ugly girl cry on the bathroom floor, thinking to myself that the world was going to end, it was actually the death of who I was. That death had to happen for the rebirth of who I was becoming. What I've learned through the years is to recognize when the "death of who I was" is starting to happen instead of trying to avoid it.

You have to grieve the pain of losing the past version of yourself to create space to look forward to stepping into the new version of who you are becoming.

Amid failure, I look around everywhere, put on a lens, and ask, *"What am I learning in this failure? What can I journal about to understand better? Why is this happening?"* If we look at it from that lens, we move through it much faster, and we don't wreak havoc on our nervous systems. You're not creating unneeded disappointment because you're embracing that with business success come peaks and valleys. Both are equally important.

When you look at the earth's landscape, there are only so many points that are actual mountaintops. When you are standing on a peak, everything appears perfect. But on each side of that peak, you're either sliding down or you're climbing up. Reaching that peak is glorious, but it's also short-lived.

How graceful can you be in the momentum of the downward slide?

How agile can you be on the climb to the next peak with the headwinds and resistance?

These are the more of the real questions that we need to ask ourselves.

If you're in this business thinking that the large majority of it should be on mountaintops, *then you're in the wrong business.* You have to embrace that the large majority of our lives are lived on a learning curve—both ups and downs. When you are on those mountain peaks, embrace and enjoy them while you're there. You can laugh and find joy in the midst of growth, rebirth, and death. One of the big keys to entrepreneurship is purely accepting what is and moving through it... **no matter what.**

———————

Reflect on a moment in your professional life that you perceived as a failure. How did this experience lead to your most significant lessons of impact? Share how you have applied these lessons to positively influence your life and the lives of others.

Coming out of last year, we grew the business by 380%. All the data suggested that moving into January, we should jump from $750,000+ launches to hitting $1,000,000 launches. However, leading up to January, I was getting signals about some teammates and partnerships that weren't operating as well as they could. I kept sweeping it under the rug, avoiding the conversation, and avoiding confronting some of the malfunctions I sensed in the business.

BECOMING THE ULTIMATE MENTOR

I also had a vision for expanding the business to maximize impact. All of that to say, we hit January and thought we had everything aligned. We doubled down and invested more than I've ever invested in my business, and the first launch of the year only generated *half* the revenue that we anticipated. The launch performed horribly.

Six months later, I'm still reflecting on what it all means. When things didn't go the way I planned them, I knew in my gut that massive learnings were coming my way. The universe was trying to shake me.

The reality is that when you're operating off of your peaks, you're not looking within. When things are going great, you're not looking to change anything about yourself or your business. At the end of last year, I called in more. I said, "Universe, give me more to carry—more structure, more team, and more support so that I can make a greater impact." I asked for that in November, and then mass disruption came in January.

An analogy I discovered through my meditations, journaling, and spiritual work is that my business is like a big tree. Like trees, there are cycles of growth. For my business, January was similar to a tree in the fall with all the dead leaves, the wind blowing, and the leaves being pulled off the tree. It was a cleansing, a shaking, and a recalibration to create space for the future growth of the new leaves that would come in the spring.

From January to June, radical changes have transpired in my business and within me. My team has doubled in size. We have some of the most incredible A-players. We've strategically shifted who we're doing business with, which has radically changed our business results. Personally, it was a reality check.

Last year, I spent so much time on my own inner spiritual growth journey and expansion of my business that I almost lost focus on prioritizing time with my family. Last year was a significant season in inner shifts and inner growth, but I needed to take my head out of the sand and look outward at the impact I was making in my family.

If you're willing to look for it, you'll find many lessons during these times of radical shaking.

I realized that I needed to go back and prioritize my family even more than I already had when I initially decided to leave corporate. It was also a time for me to get even closer and grow my relationship with my husband of 15 years.

It's hard for me to articulate the number of lessons I've learned, from the perceived failure of our first goal in January 2024 to navigating all the unexpected turns this season of change has brought me. In reflection, I'm really proud of how I've navigated it, leaning on the skills I've gained to go inward, asking the hard questions about the lessons, and maintaining humility when my ego was being deconstructed during this season.

The reason I've been able to manage the cash flow in the business this year with unexpected missed goals is because, 2 years ago, when I had a million dollars, I was in the red. I didn't know how to manage the money, and I didn't know how to forecast. I didn't know how to map it out. It felt like the end of the world, but it was preparing me for the spiral up for the next time it happened. And it's not going to be the last time that it happens.

Entrepreneurship is characterized by an ebb and flow. As we hike across the mountains, we have to anticipate the valleys and plan for them. The mass disappointment in January created an opportunity for inward reflection and an operational outward look at my business. It's radically changed my business and helped me refocus on my family.

Now, we're crushing it. The business is doing great, and we're operating radically differently than how we did the first half of this year. Had the perceived failure not happened in January, I wouldn't have made the changes to my business I needed to make, *because I wouldn't have been looking for them*. Had January not happened, I wouldn't have gone to work to recalibrate my availability and priorities with my children and my spouse. I wouldn't have re-assessed how I communicate and lead my team, and we wouldn't have reached the new level of growth we've achieved as a company.

I needed to evolve into the leader the company needed me to become, and I needed to evolve to the next level of mother and spouse my family needed me to become.

Failure is *not* a bad thing. Failure forces you to go within and do what's necessary to allow rebirth.

How do you ensure your business practices align with ethical and sustainable principles while balancing profitability with making a positive impact?

It always goes back to that gut check of, "What is the purpose of this?" I ask myself questions like: *"Is it going to provide value for our clients?"* or *"Will it create a positive impact on the collective?"*

If you've been involved in anything we produce, you know we pride ourselves on over-delivering. To this day, people can't believe how much value we give in our free programs. Similarly, once they enroll in our paid programs, they're astonished at the amount of support and coaching they receive.

We brought in an experienced marketing team this year, and it's funny because they say, based on industry standards, that our company is giving so much more than the average program similar to ours. They've asked if we've considered dialing things back, but **we're not here to be the industry standard. We're here to drive results and impact for people.** I would much rather be known for being a company that goes above and beyond, rather than one that lured you into something that you were wildly disappointed for.

I believe in being in business for the long haul. This means surprising and delighting your clients so that they stay around for a lifetime. If you burn and churn and only focus on profits, you will constantly be looking for new customers due to low retention.

Now, surprising and delighting your clients is ethical. From a practical, sustainable business angle, *there is no better and easier sell than retaining current clients.* If you've done your job by overdelivering in the first place, the conversion rate with a current client is astronomically higher than going out to the cold market and trying to sell someone something new. That's just Business 101.

Now, let's talk about impact. The best way to drive those sales is to give the most value and transformation in their first experience with you. Whether I'm driven for profit or value, you could argue either way that I'll only get profit in the ascension model if I surprise, delight, and give value to my clients when they first come in. That's how we balance impact with profit.

If you impact them, you'll create more profit.

Impact=Income

What role do partnerships and collaborations play in amplifying the impact of your business? How do you identify and cultivate meaningful relationships with other business leaders?

Without collaborations and partnerships, I wouldn't be where I am today or even an eighth of where I am today. I say this all the time—"Your network is your net worth."

I learned that early on—it's not just about taking from others. It's a rule of reciprocity. Get into rooms and ask yourself, *"What gifts do I have that I can give others and vice versa?"* Some people make the mistake of getting into rooms and only thinking about what they can gain. But that's wrong. It's a two-way street. It's a yin and yang of getting each other visibility and raising each other up in your own communities.

Relationships and partnerships are, bar none, the number one key to success in business.

You can know all the strategies and have the best offer ever, but if you're not connected to the right people and the right network, you're not selling anything.

Mutual advocacy is another huge benefit of partnerships and collaborations. My business took off because my mentors, who are well-known in the industry, were advocates for me. They put me on their podcasts. They saw the gaps in my business and connected me to others who could help fill those.

There is no more valuable asset in your business than your network. To this day, in every program I run, the reason we bring so much value is because of the network I've surrounded myself with.

Looking ahead, what are your aspirations for your business's future impact, and how do you plan to continue evolving and innovating in this area?

I have big dreams. I believe in a 360 approach to business. That's why our mastermind is called Elevate 360. I mentor this approach and see it evolve within our mastermind members every year.

In the first couple of months, we do a lot of intense inner work. It's not uncommon for some of them to resist it. They ask, "Why do I need this? I just need to grow my business." Undoubtedly, though, I get messages saying, "Oh my gosh. I didn't realize how blocked I was. I didn't realize how much a certain relationship held me back in business. I didn't realize how this piece in my past has impacted X, Y, Z."

I truly believe that **bodies build businesses.** Less than 5% of businesses make it to the million-dollar-a-year mark. Yes, business strategy is important, but I wouldn't have been able to experience this success had I not cleared the path in my nervous system to embrace it and roll with the turbulence along the way.

This goes back to the idea of moving through failure. What makes or breaks an entrepreneur is their ability to be resilient. Your ability to be resilient often depends on the tools in your tool belt, and many entrepreneurs just don't have them yet.

It's sad because you often see entrepreneurs with a great product or idea, but their business falls apart because they don't have the capacity to manage it and overcome the unpredictable headwinds that inevitably happen.

My high-in-the-sky, big dream is to create even more elevated experiential retreats that focus on this 360-degree approach. I'll always have my Elevate 360 year-long mastermind, but we are actively creating new in-person experiences to get more business owners the tools they need to move through the challenges and develop lives where happiness, health, and wealth are all equally achieved.

We are in the process of building a luxury mountain home. We intend to use this property to host intensive retreats where we'll teach the skills necessary to live all out through this 360 approach to entrepreneurship. We're going to roll up our sleeves and get to work on your business plan. We're going to literally run the numbers and build out your strategy for the year, which a lot of entrepreneurs still need to do. I'm also going to have you on the floor, doing breathwork, meditating, crying, and working through all the baggage that's holding you back.

My goal is to become the ultimate mentor. Let me be clear, though, that it is not just about raising myself to that elevated position. I live by the JFK quote, "A rising tide lifts all boats." My vision is to always collaborate with the best experts in the energy and somatic field, with me serving as the catalyst that makes it possible for more people to experience their gifting. I am not going to facilitate everything; rather, it will be more like a beehive with many different people serving in many different roles, all working towards one main goal—

To make an all-out impact on the community at large.

"LEADERSHIP IS NOT ABOUT GIVING
ENERGY. IT IS ABOUT UNLEASHING OTHER
PEOPLE'S ENERGY."

Paul Polman

first, from within

JULIE COBER

in /juliecober

juliecober.com

Julie is a former Fortune 100 Chief Resources Officer and now the Founder & CEO of the Legacy Leadership Academy for Women. She is a Certified Master Leadership Coach that works with female entrepreneurs and professionals and provides transformational business, career and mindset coaching with a focus on clarity of purpose, depth of impact, and what it means to lead from within.

What sets Julie apart in the Business Leadership Coaching space is her deep understanding of what it takes to succeed without the persistent overwhelm and constant sacrifice. She leads, guides, supports and shares her years of successful experience in goal setting, team building, executing strategy and facilitating results quickly.

How do you define impact?

As a Leadership Coach and Mentor, I know I've made an impact when the women I work with learn to lead in all aspects of their lives and always *First From Within.*

The impact we build together leads her to believe in herself, step into the greatest version of herself, and live a life she loves waking up to every single day.

This often starts in her professional life, either in building her business or career, and then quickly moves to all aspects of her life—health, relationships, money, and more.

To me, impact is when a woman can re-discover her true, authentic self and show up every single day knowing who she is and what she's here to accomplish. In my business, we call this *The Assignment.*

So many of us, myself included, have looked externally to ourselves for success, validation, approval, love, or recognition for years. It's so common, and it's so unfulfilling. Impact is when you learn to go within and know that every answer you seek is already within you; the work is to get quiet, listen intently, and tap into your intuition.

That's when you know you're making an impact.

Looking back over your life, who has impacted you most, and what specific advice or guidance from them has not only influenced your personal growth but also significantly impacted the direction of your professional career?

The person who has impacted me the most in my life is my oldest brother, Kevin, and not in a way that most would talk about this topic.

We grew up in a nice, middle-class home with three kids. He's the oldest, and I'm the youngest. My mom stayed home with us, and my dad went to work— probably like most families in our time (the 1970s). At the time, I thought my childhood was great, but there was always this constant conflict happening in our house that we learned to tolerate and didn't discuss— caused by my brother.

He was troubled (I understand this now). When we were kids, though, I didn't understand why he was the way he was. He's five years older than me and we always had a very volatile relationship. He was mean. He was angry. He was a bully, and he said terrible things to all of us often. Because I was the youngest, I was most often his target. Truth be told, when we were growing up, I remember often thinking how much I hated him. Because of who he was and the things he would do, I secretly often felt unsafe in my own home.

Now, as an adult, that has spent years working on myself and the mental trauma I experienced through Kevin, what I know clearly is that he was just a really scared little boy, and he was hurt. His fear and hurt were projected onto me and my family. What I know to my core now, through growing up with Kevin, is that *hurt people... hurt people.*

It was never about me. Kevin was and is my *Contrast.* My polar opposite.

My brother taught me what unkindness truly looks like. Through those experiences, I discovered my core values, developed very strong leadership and decision-making skills, and learned how to be very resilient in all aspects of my life. For this, I am actually extremely grateful for the contrast he caused. I fully understand that this was necessary to become the version of me that I am today.

I've enjoyed a very successful career both as an HR Executive and now CEO of my own Leadership

Coaching Company, and for that, I can now actually empathize with and thank my brother.

How did I get to where I am today? A ton of inner work and forgiveness. I now know exactly why he behaves the way he behaves, and I actually had the same feelings at times in my life. We were both trying to get attention. We just went about it in very different ways.

The journey to today has been very impactful in many ways, and now I am proud of the very strong boundaries I've set when it comes to my brother.

When all is said and done, I'm happy to say that I sit in deep gratitude for him and all the contrast he caused because it has played a key role in shaping me into who I am today.

Think about the personal challenges you've overcome in your life. How did the obstacles that you've overcome play a part in the impact that you make now?

Because of the personal conflict I mentioned above, I started to believe I wasn't good enough when I was younger. This core limiting belief took hold and started to show up in other areas of my life—most predominantly in my career.

Before I started my own business, I worked in corporate Canada for 28 years. I worked extremely hard and climbed the corporate mountain in Human Resources and reached what I would describe as my summit. When I left corporate at the end of 2019, I was the Chief Human Resources Officer of a very large organization. I'd done it. Reached the top of my game, but quickly realized I didn't love what I was doing. My heart and soul told me, for years, that this is the wrong path! Sadly, I didn't listen because I was on a quest. A quest to feel good enough. A quest to finally feel good enough in the eyes of my dad. To finally make my dad proud.

Fast-forward to 2010, at the peak of my career, my world was turned upside down, which I now clearly see was a pivotal turning point in my life. My husband Daryl was diagnosed with non-Hodgkin's lymphoma. He was 41. It was an aggressive cancer that needed to be treated quickly and aggressively. So we went on this journey, and the rest of that year was a blur. I was just trying to survive through it, keeping up appearances, making sure everyone knew I was okay when I wasn't. Ensuring everyone thought I was good enough to do it all, while I supported my husband through the most difficult time in his life, our life.

Thankfully now, 14 years later, he's fine. He's been in remission for years, and he's doing amazing.

The journey of 2010 (we had a few other major life events hit our family that year) was not only the biggest personal challenge I'd faced up to that point, but it also started me on my quest to go within, to figure out what this core negative limiting belief of never feeling good enough was all about and how I could change it.

The time I spent in achieving a career I didn't fully love and the personal challenge of facing and fighting a grave health challenge led me to decide enough was enough. Change was necessary for me to live my life the way I truly wanted to—happy, fulfilled, at peace, and making a true Impact. I needed new life tools, and new tools is what I found.

I would have loved to have had these powerful mindset tools that I now teach when I was trying to 'manage my life' back then, but I now know I wasn't meant to have them then. I was meant to experience the contrast. I was meant to learn and grow exactly how I did and still do today.

We all experience challenges. It's an important part of life. Just know that there are tools that will help you through, and you have them, right now, today, within you. You will face peaks and valleys in life. Know that the valleys are your contrast, and they come for everyone. The valleys are our teachers. They come with a purpose. They are important, and they will pass, no matter how challenging.

———————

Reflect on a moment in your professional life that you perceived as a failure. How did this experience lead to your most significant lessons of impact? Share how you have applied these lessons to positively influence your life and the lives of others.

Although I knew for years that I wasn't fulfilled by my career and the success I was enjoying, it still took 13 years to muster up the courage to actually leave my J.O.B.

I knew I wanted to do something different. I wanted to work for myself. I wanted "time freedom." I already had financial freedom. It wasn't about money.

IT WAS ABOUT BALANCE, MAKING AN IMPACT, AND LIVING A LIFE I TRULY LOVED WAKING UP TO EVERY DAY.

It was about balance, making an impact, and living a life I truly loved waking up to every day.

For years, my career was the nucleus of our family. Every decision was made around whether it would 'fit' within the requirements of my job.

I wanted this to change. I wanted my family to be the nucleus, and every decision revolved around them. If it wasn't right for my family, then we aren't doing it. For 13 years, I kept trying to leave and do different things. I started network marketing companies. I went and did some HR Leadership 'gig' work, and I hit what I called my upper limit.

If you're sitting in a room, you can see the ceiling. Your upper limit is your ceiling. The goal is to make your ceiling your new floor so that you're constantly growing and expanding. Often when people hit their upper limit, their ceiling, they start to unconsciously self-sabotage because they start to feel very uncomfortable. This was me.

Every time I tried to go out on my own, I was getting too close to my upper limit. I would self-sabotage and go back to my comfort zone. Where I felt most safe. I felt safe as a corporate executive, even though it was 'sucking the life out of me.'

Then I got fired.

For someone who struggled with the feelings of 'never being good enough,' you can imagine what being fired felt like.

I was mortified, and I felt shame, embarrassment, and confusion. I'd always been considered a 'top talent,' and I wondered, *"How did this happen?"*

Pretty quickly, after again going within and really reflecting, I realized I wasn't giving it my all in this job.

Deep down, I wanted to leave. I knew what my exit package would give me in severance. I'm pretty certain I wanted this to happen on some level so that I could finally make the leap.

At the time, I thought this was my biggest failure ever. Now I know it was my biggest blessing. I was free—free to be me.

I had been telling the universe what I wanted for years. It gave me many opportunities, but I kept going back. My soul told me my corporate life wasn't my path. I knew it wasn't what I was here to do. It wasn't my assignment. I just needed a push, and the universe took over.

It took me years, but finally, by the end of 2019, I

decided to do it. Switching from being an employee for 28 years to an entrepreneur was hard, but today, as I imagined, I'm making way more impact. I took the risk and finally broke my upper limit.

Now, my ceiling is my floor.

How do you ensure your business practices align with ethical and sustainable principles while balancing profitability with making a positive impact?

Intuition is one of the six 'superpowers' we've been given, and as a successful leader and CEO, I tap into it daily to run my business ethically, aligned with my heart, and profitably. Your intuition is one of the most important tools you have as a leader and business owner.

From that perspective, I don't do things in my business that don't *FEEL* right. I make decisions daily, and I make them quickly, and they're always the output of reflection and intuition. Mastering this superpower has been the biggest change for me, going from an employee to an entrepreneur. In corporate, I would say I lived way more 'in my head.' As a successful business owner, I now live way more 'in my heart.'

To tap into your intuition, you start by defining and designing your goals—who you want to be and how you want to show up. You become aware of your thoughts and whether they're serving you or not.

What decisions do you make and why?

What are you saying to yourself about yourself all day long?

You script out the version of yourself that you want to be and then start being that person. Start practicing who you want to become and make decisions from that mindset.

Understand the impact you want to make and tap into your intuition as to who you need to BE and what you need to DO to make that impact and influence happen. You get to choose the version of you that you want to BE.

Be that person NOW.

What role do partnerships and collaborations play in amplifying the impact of your business? How do you identify and cultivate meaningful relationships with other business leaders?

Partnerships and collaborations are huge, especially for entrepreneurs, because entrepreneurship can be lonely. If you have an online business, your team can be located around the world. It's essential to get into the right rooms. You never want to be the smartest person in the room because when you are, you've outgrown the room and won't continue to grow or learn.

Build community, find partnerships, get and give support, and attend live events when you can. Get into the rooms that will push you to grow.

When you come across a new contact, always remember, you'll never know how you are impacting them and how they may impact you.

My dad gave me a great piece of advice early in my career in terms of impact. He said, Julie, always be kind because those you meet and connect with on your rise, you will likely cross paths again on the way down.

What my dad meant was to go above and beyond and always leave people with an impression of increase. This is how you make an impact and build meaningful relationships, partnerships, and collaborations.

———————————

Looking ahead, what are your aspirations for the future impact of your business, and how do you plan to continue evolving and innovating in this area?

I was at a live event recently and realized why I've been feeling so uncomfortable lately. I'm ascending in my awareness and in the midst of a quantum leap.

One of our philosophies in my business is that we meet women where they're at. Our goal is to always be creating offers that match where they are today and where they want to go.

My vision for new offers, to add to our current suite, revolves around:

More Community
More Connection
More Collaboration.

More ways to bring amazing, like-minded women together through things like masterminds, VIP days, and retreats.

I am doing more speaking, launching a podcast, and envisioning bigger stages. My goal is to get as visible as possible, so I can share these life-changing leadership and mindset tools with as many women as possible.

I believe that everyone deserves to love their life—to be fulfilled and happy, and to be aware of who they are and why they're here.

I will continue to push myself to grow and evolve my leadership, mindset, and awareness so that I can continue to support, guide, and mentor women to believe in themselves, step into their greatness, and live a life they love waking up to each and every day— by *First Going Within*.

hope dealer

DARLA BONK

in /darlabonkconsulting

darlabonk.com

I ignite

M motivate

P propel

A amplify

C cultivate

T transform

Darla is a compassionate and highly sought-after management and business consultant who leads, equips, and trains CEOs, Entrepreneurs, and C-Suite Executives to fall in love with their businesses again through her B.A.L.L. out method—BUILD. AND. LIVE the LIFE you love.

She effectively leads businesses through investing in leadership development, systems, methods, and processes to generate revenue, increase profitability, and improve performance.

With over 20 years of executive, corporate, and leadership experience, including building a business with her husband from scratch to running a successful company with 15 employees and generating multiple seven figures annually, Darla is leading the way in how businesses should operate and how leaders should lead.

Darla resides in Fort Myers, Florida, with her husband, Jeff. They have four grown children and enjoy traveling and seeing the world.

How do you define impact?

Impact is the influence that is made so strongly on others that it compels them to take action to bring about a change in their current circumstance.

When I think back to people in my life who had an impact on me, I was not just moved by what they were doing or saying, but I was compelled to change my circumstances based on what I saw.

Impact is the ability to influence the world around us by helping people improve their circumstances, even if that starts with helping them believe it's possible.

First, you have to believe it can be done, then decide to do something about it. You have to create or take massive action to create a massive impact.

To take that massive action, you have to realize that your circumstances can be changed. Never assume that people don't need you; always look for ways to help.

One of the people I love is journalist Hoda Kotb. She always says, "Look for the helpers." Regardless of your status—financially or socially—if you can make an impact, you must do so.

Helping others is fueled by my belief in Christ and my knowledge of what I was put on this earth to do.

Who I am in Christ allows me to know what to say, when to say it, and how to say it so that you see there is hope in the world. I love it when people tell me, "You're a hope dealer. You're an encourager." That has nothing to do with me but everything to do with who Jesus is in me, whether it's through business interactions, being a wife, friend, etc.

IMPACT is the ability to ignite the passion in others, motivate them to take action, propel them to find unwavering focus, amplify their potential, cultivate the environment for them to be successful, and transform an organization through effective leadership.

Looking back over your life, who has impacted you most, and what specific advice or guidance from them has not only influenced your personal growth but also significantly impacted the direction of your professional career?

My dad was a pastor for 35 years, and he always made sure that we heard him say, "I love you," every day.

He told us how beautiful we were and that we could accomplish anything. He has always been my biggest supporter.

Yet, I struggled to believe I was good enough to be worthy of my parents' love.

I also struggled to believe I was good enough to be worthy of God's love for me—not because of anything my parents had taught me. It wasn't the typical, "Oh, I never heard this from my parents." It was the complete opposite. I grew up in the perfect family environment. But inside, I couldn't believe it.

My daddy was also a mover and a shaker. In addition to being a pastor, he was on the radio weekly, and he was a singer. He had albums, and he wrote dozens of books. I saw a fabulous work ethic in him, and I saw that if you're good at something, you need to utilize that talent that God gave you.

He always said, "Give God your absolute best. God gave his best." If I can do something that can help people, then I need to find a way to make it work.

He created that influence and impact, and not just as a pastor or singer.

It helped me realize, as an entrepreneur, that it doesn't have to be just one thing. As long as it aligns with who you are, what you're trying to accomplish, and who you're trying to serve, it can be incredibly impactful.

He was the first person that I saw consistently and generously pour back into the people in whom he was investing. He didn't do things to get to a better financial position or just because it was "the right thing to do."

He also made us citizens of the world. We traveled the world. Politics and religion were okay to talk about if you could do it respectfully.

Knowing to have critical conversations on sensitive topics made me learn how to communicate with other people. I love being able to find out, "Tell me why that is?" It can bring us

LET ME SEEK TO UNDERSTAND BEFORE I ASK TO BE UNDERSTOOD.

closer together. Conflict is just a great way to bring connection; it's a great way to bridge the chasm of what divides us. It doesn't mean I have to change my beliefs. Let me seek to understand before I ask to be understood.

Think about the personal challenges you've overcome in your life. How did the obstacles that you've overcome play a part in the impact that you make now?

When people hear my story, they don't understand why I don't have regrets. Without the experiences, I wouldn't have learned any lessons.

My family upbringing was wonderful, but some difficult experiences gave me a better understanding of the world around me. It allowed me to approach people with compassion and empathy. It helped me find a way to connect with people wherever they are, no matter who they are.

One of many choices that I made along the way was getting pregnant and having a child before marriage.

For me, an abortion was not the outcome I wanted, given the fact that I found myself in a less-than-stellar situation. The beautiful thing is that 26 years later, God has allowed me to share my story with others. Having gone through that experience, I completely understand and respect the choices others make for themselves.

Given that my choices didn't necessarily honor him in those days, God has allowed me to use those experiences to be a tool to connect to people who feel isolated and ostracized. You have no idea how people feel or how they end up in the situations they are in. You don't know their story.

The first thing you can do to help somebody else is to lead with understanding. It doesn't mean you have to agree with everything that has happened, but because I have allowed God to heal me from past situations, it has given me more compassion and love towards people. If I had not gone through some of these tough circumstances in my life, I would have said, "I don't know what's wrong with you. Fix your mess. You did this to yourself." But because I found myself in various situations that were less than ideal, I have a heart for people that others have turned their backs on.

Everybody has a past, AND everybody has a future. You want people to extend grace and see you for what you can be when you're not at your best. So why would you not do the same for other people?

It's cool to watch all the ways that God allows you to be a beacon of light for somebody else.

Reflect on a moment in your professional life that you perceived as a failure. How did this experience lead to your most significant lessons of impact? Share how you have applied these lessons to positively influence your life and the lives of others.

After 90 days of working for a private FinTech company, my direct boss asked me, "Where do you want to be in five years?" I said, "I want to be sitting in your seat." I thought that was a great answer (and I meant it!). He did not think that was a good answer. In fact, his whole approach to me moving forward changed in a very cold way.

I learned a great lesson: not everyone that you work with will be in your corner. Some people will try to snuff out your light, but you can't let them do that.

I am the driver of my success. It's not up to a company to make me rich or to give me a position.

I also realized that I don't care about titles; I care about impact.

At that time, my now-husband and I started talking about starting a company. It created an all-or-nothing mindset. We decided to make it work, and we did.

Eight years later, our company has 15 employees. We've helped employees buy cars or a home. We've helped people fix their credit. Being able to have the influence and lift up, build, and restore those who are in my charge, well... that wasn't my experience with someone whose charge I was in.

You are created as a masterpiece and have a very specific and unique purpose. You may not know what that purpose is at this time, but every situation you encounter and go through until you walk into it will prepare you for when you realize your purpose. You have everything you need in the toolkit to make you equipped to stand firm and confident, knowing, "I don't need anybody else's approval."

I don't need them to say, "Okay, you can have my seat." I'm going to create the seat because I have a Creator who already gave me everything I needed inside of me to make that seat happen all by myself.

It was a lesson learned in a negative way where I said (to myself), "Thank you very much. Watch what I do."

How do you ensure your business practices align with ethical and sustainable principles while balancing profitability with making a positive impact?

My ace in the pocket is God. My faith drives absolutely everything that I do: my priorities, my business, and my personal life all drive around my faith.

Everything that I do goes through the Holy Spirit sifter. He determines what I get to do, and what I don't get to do.

I trust and believe that God's plan for me is better than any dream I've ever had. He knows me. He made me. Why would I not trust him?

My ethics and integrity align with God's word—it's the essence of who I am if I am a follower of Christ. I don't want to do anything that would ever break his heart. It's a relationship that moves and guides everything that I do.

I pray about the finances of the business. It's an unpopular opinion, even among Christian business owners that I'm friends with, but I tithe on my business. God's never going to owe you money. He's never going to owe you a dime. I don't just tithe what I pay myself. The very first check I pay is my tithe to God. I'll pay myself a basic wage that works, put away money for taxes, and then reinvest back into the business so I can better myself for my people or create a better impact.

When you trust God with everything, even your business, he will never owe you. If you operate your business in a sound way with strategic business practices, you shouldn't have to worry about money.

I have specific financial goals that have nothing to do with my husband and me. Those goals will change multiple people's lives, and they might just allow them to have hope again—maybe even believe there is something and someone worth believing in again in this world. That's what gets me up in the morning.

People impact people, not money.

What role do partnerships and collaborations play in amplifying the impact of your business? How do you identify and cultivate meaningful relationships with other business leaders?

What is your company's WHY? Unless you're an Elon Musk type, there's not a unique product offering that any of us have. Why did you get in? Why did you start your business? What did you want this business to do?

I think it goes back to finding your MAC team—Who are your Mentors? Who are your Allies? Who are your Champions?

Maybe my community could benefit from a collaboration or partnership. Do we have mutually desired goals? Are we aligned in what we are trying to accomplish for our clients? Do we both want to serve our clients well in a way that generates a better life for them and creates a bigger impact? Do we have similar approaches to our systems, processes, and results?

If there's an opportunity. Great. But just because there's an opportunity doesn't mean it's the right opportunity.

I might like or even love you. You might be somebody I'm friends with for the rest of my life, but that doesn't mean I'm going to trust you on the business front. I think it's okay to also ask those questions just like you would in dating.

Whether it's on being on each other's podcast or offering a product to coincide with your service or vice versa... whether we're co-authoring a book together... the question is, does this create a bigger impact in the world around us?

It's worthwhile to go through a litany of questions to determine, "Does this make sense? Or am I just a supporter of your business from the sidelines?"

If Tony Robbins calls you tomorrow and wants you to collaborate on his business, would you say no to that? I very well might if it doesn't align with what I'm trying to do. The second you start getting your eyes on the glory, the next big stage or big name, you have missed it entirely.

———————

Looking ahead, what are your aspirations for the future impact of your business, and how do you plan to continue evolving and innovating in this area?

I am a business management consultant also doing some executive coaching per request, but I have not been selling that. I recently had a literal come-to-Jesus meeting where God said, "You have had too many experiences, and have learned and healed too much, to not share with more people this offer."

It has always been easier for me to find what's wrong with a business rather than walk through life with the owners. I didn't want to do that because "everybody's a coach."

Now, I am excited and passionate about getting into coaching hard and soft skills. I'm probably going to do those in front of a live audience and maximize the impact of our podcast (On Your Way business podcast). I look at it as a legacy project to encourage others to know that they have everything they need to be everything they were created to be. I want to compound the impact.

If one little thing I do helps others take that next step to catapult the journey that they were designed for, great. If that means that all I ever did was plant a seed and never see the harvest, that's okay, too. But you'll never see the harvest if somebody didn't first plant the seed. If all I ever am is a seed planter, so be it. I've done my job.

"IF YOUR ACTIONS CREATE A LEGACY THAT INSPIRES OTHERS TO DREAM MORE, LEARN MORE, DO MORE AND BECOME MORE, THEN, YOU ARE AN EXCELLENT LEADER."

Dolly Parton

the power of
intentional impact

ANNIE MIRZA

/anniemirza

sensus.social

Annie Mirza is a CPA turned digital marketing strategist, website designer, and business coach for Accountants.

As the founder of Sensus Social, she coaches accountants on a holistic approach to building human-focused digital firms that they can be proud to leave as their legacy.

Her transition from a burned-out accountant to a successful online business strategist serves as a testament to her commitment to reshaping the accounting industry norms. Annie's mission is to show accountants there's another way to build a firm that gives you freedom of time, money, and purpose.

Outside of her role as the CEO, Annie's passions are just as multifaceted and include writing fiction, training for a Taekwondo black belt, embarking on exciting family adventures across the world, spending Saturdays with her parents, and trying, albeit at times unsuccessful, to learn how to ski with her kids.

———

How do you define impact?

We are constantly impacting one another, even as strangers passing in the street. So, we should be intentional about how we interact with others.

When you've achieved success, it only makes sense to share it with people around you. We don't live in silos; we live in communities. So when we rise, everyone else rises with us.

———

Looking back over your life, who has impacted you most, and what specific advice or guidance from them has not only influenced your personal growth but also significantly impacted the direction of your professional career?

Looking back, I can see moments in life—threads that define my life. I've gone through a very complex journey.

One moment that has always come back to me is something my grandfather said when I was very young. I spent a lot of time with my grandparents during the summer months. My mom was a teacher, and we would visit my grandparents when she had school holidays. We would often hang out with my granddad, who was retired.

When my brother and I would hang out with him, he would share his wisdom about different things that were going on in his life. He poured his beliefs, values, and ideals about God, life, people, and relationships into us. He didn't know what kind of impact he was leaving on us.

We were young—just ten and nine years old when he passed away—but we were very impressionable. Sometimes people wonder, *"Little kids? They're not even listening?"* But I believe we do absorb things, and they stay with us in our subconscious.

One memory that still resonates with me today and has profoundly impacted my life is how my grandfather spoke about my future compared to my brother's.

My brother was a typical boy who got into everything, while I was quiet, observant, and a rule follower.

I can still hear it clear as day: he said, "My baby is going to grow up to become a doctor. When she walks out, people are going to stand up for her." As for my brother, he said, "You're going to sell corn on a street cart."

He didn't say this maliciously; it was an innocent remark to a little boy who wasn't listening. But, when you're growing up in a male-dominated society like Pakistan, hearing "you can do better than a boy" planted a seed of confidence.

Ironically, my brother grew up to become a highly sought-after vascular surgeon, and I became a CPA.

But for my grandfather, it wasn't just empty words. He treated women in our family like royalty, with utter respect and priority. He raised my mother and aunt as strong and independent women. He valued their opinions, never raised his voice, and encouraged and supported them.

My grandfather's words and beliefs carried as "my truth" and gave me the confidence to fight the world.

His teachings remain with me, and I see them through the influence of my mom and her entire family—my uncles, my aunt, their children, everyone.

Having lived in a very male-dominated society and then later moved to the U.S., where I became my own person while going through college and later entering a male-dominated accounting industry, those words helped me in many ways. My grandad's philosophies, way of life, beliefs, and ideas about how to treat people and how to have strong, uncompromising values helped me navigate a complex world.

As an accountant, I audited multibillion-dollar companies, so you must have your values set. Integrity and ethics are important in that field. So my grandad had a lot of impact on me, even the very little time that I got to spend with him. I still think about him every single day.

———————

Think about the personal challenges you've overcome in your life. How did the obstacles that you've overcome play a part in the impact that you make now?

One of my biggest challenges is definitely what made me who I am today. Everything we experience leaves an impact on us and becomes part of our story, but for me, moving to Australia was extremely challenging.

My family was my "safety blanket." My family protected me during my childhood in Pakistan. Home became the place of safety where I felt comfortable. The outside world was chaos, but at home, I could be myself. My family gave me the comfort and resources I needed—along with a lot of love and affection.

As a young woman in Pakistan, it was very difficult to go outside because you were teased. You'd hear, "Hey pretty, what's your name?" It was normal to get harassed by guys, so I became very isolated inside our home.

However, I moved to the U.S. when I was 17 and experienced newfound freedom. If guys were interested in you, they would politely ask for your number. If I said, "No," they would walk away. I never felt like I had to constantly defend myself.

My parents gave me so much freedom in the U.S. My dad got me a car and taught me how to drive. He got me a cell phone and told me to call him if I needed help. That was the opposite of how I lived in Pakistan.

With this new freedom, I realized that I was capable of so much more than who I was in Pakistan. I felt I could do anything.

I was working with a big accounting firm when I got married. Because my husband was in I.T. and was super smart, he got many job offers from all over the world. He asked me where I would like to move, and Australia was one of our options.

Honestly, the only thing I knew about Australia was that it is another continent, but we decided to go and start a new life there.

When I told my accounting firm I would be moving, they started putting me on random jobs that didn't give me any experience, even though I had worked there for a whole year. It was fair enough for the company, but I didn't gain the experience I needed for an entire year.

Moving to Australia was a big change. First, my family was taken away, which was my safety and my protection. My everything. On top of that, the demands of my new job in Australia put extreme constraints on my relationship and emotional well-being.

In general, it was a very different culture, environment, and expectations. Everything became too much. I knew I had to figure things out, but when life is pulled from under you, you tend to think you're alone and no one can help you.

Reflect on a moment in your professional life that you perceived as a failure. How did this experience lead to your most significant lessons of impact? Share how you have applied these lessons to positively influence your life and the lives of others.

Working in the accounting industry had many challenges. First, I worked too many hours. I brought work home, managed the household, and studied for my U.S. CPA exams (which was like a full-time job on its own). Plus, there was so much going on within the work environment.

One of the biggest things I struggled with was the corporate culture and politics. I wasn't cut out for that. I stayed in my lane, but it was cumbersome and exhausting.

I pushed through it for as long as I could, but when I decided to have a family, I knew I couldn't continue. Leaving was the only option that I saw. I could not continue to work like that and raise a family.

I had different ideas of how I wanted to raise my kids. I wanted to raise them with my values. I wanted to teach them everything from developing healthy eating habits to how to see the world through their own eyes, so I knew I had to do that myself, and daycare wasn't an option.

Still, it wasn't an easy decision for somebody who had so much success in her career despite the struggles to leave the corporate world behind.

THE TURNING POINT WAS WHEN I NOTICED SUCCESSFUL BUSINESSES THAT FAILED BECAUSE THEY HAD POOR FINANCE MANAGEMENT.

When I decided to go back to work, I didn't want anything to do with the accounting industry at first. We had a consulting business and passion projects we wanted to grow. I knew that I had to learn marketing. So, I did. When I'd meet my friends who were still in accounting, they would ask me, "How do you do marketing?" When I'd share, they'd say, "We need you in the accounting industry."

Accountants don't know how to market themselves. They don't know how to sell their services outside of referrals, which is what they always rely on. This kept coming back to me, though I resisted for as long as I could.

The turning point was when I noticed successful businesses that failed because they had poor finance management.

I realized that accountants are not just needed; they're essential to this economy.

To help others, I had to relive all of my accounting experiences. I asked myself, "What are the things that I struggled with?" Then, I asked myself, "How can I help accountants get out of that and market themselves?"

That's how I created my business.

In my professional opinion, foundations in organic marketing strategies are essential for expansion. Now, I help accountants set strong foundations by creating an incredible online presence that not only builds their authority but serves as their marketing backend.

I help them create an organic marketing strategy. I help build their confidence. I coach them to show up as their best selves online. If you don't believe in yourself, then nobody else is going to believe in you.

People are so burned out that they think leaving is the only solution, but it's not. We need more accountants in the industry. I want people to see that there is a way to have a balanced life. The online marketplace is full of opportunities; you just need to know what will work for your unique business and skill set.

One of my missions is to help others grow a business that gives them freedom of time, money, and purpose. If your business becomes the same thing that caused you to burn out in the first place, then there's no point in it. I want you to build a business that sustains you and gives you a purposeful life.

———

How do you ensure your business practices align with ethical and sustainable principles while balancing profitability with making a positive impact?

Marketing is a place where there's a lot of skepticism because there are people who will do anything to make a few bucks. I always filter marketing through the lens of my integrity and my values.

I ask, "Is this in alignment with what I would do for myself? Would I be able to sleep at night if I did this? Is this the value I want to pass on to my kids? Is this how I want people to perceive me? Is this my identity?"

I believe that we don't just live on earth for a while, and then we're done. I believe in the afterlife, and how we live here will decide how we will live in the next life. I don't want to compromise my values and integrity for money. It's not worth it.

My work is always filtered through my subconscious. In seconds, it passes through a sieve of values and integrity, and then it comes out the other side. Is it a yes, or is it a no? Am I making this decision just for me, or will it help people? Is it going to be helpful to their businesses?

Making money is simple and easy if you understand how it works. Bring value to other people, and they will compensate you accordingly. The more value you can bring, and the better you can communicate that value to others, the more money you can make. That's what I focus on in my marketing for my own businesses and for my clients.

What role do partnerships and collaborations play in amplifying the impact of your business? How do you identify and cultivate meaningful relationships with other business leaders?

Relationships are extremely important. I intended to build a community for accountants where they could all come together and become a resource for each other, not just a place for me to sell something to them. Having a strong community is a powerful thing to have in a business.

Giving back to a community is rewarding in itself, but collaborating in a way that helps others works as a multiplier. If you can align your business with another that shares your values, you can form a powerful alliance that will benefit both of your clients, resulting in more people benefiting.

Being a business owner is hard, so it also helps to find other people who are going through the same thing.

There will also be people who will not rise with you, and you'll need to let them go. It's hard, especially if they're close to you, but it is something that you have to come to peace with. If you stay down with them, you're robbing all the other people of your magic. When you rise, others might see the possibility and think they might have a chance. It's not a selfish act to cut ties with a person if they're not willing to rise with you.

Who knows? By the time you reach the level you desire, those people might be inspired and come back into the relationship. Sometimes you have to let go of friendships that you've outgrown—and that's okay.

Looking ahead, what are your aspirations for the future impact of your business, and how do you plan to continue evolving and innovating in this area?

I'm a dreamer. I have big plans for my businesses and the accounting industry. I see it moving in a very positive direction. Collectively, we have a strong base to make a change in the industry. That's why I invested in volunteering in the local CPA societies— because they're connected to the decision-makers.

We are identifying the things that need to change in the industry. I'm trying to see things from both levels: from the legislation and also from the view of people who are in the thick of it. We are trying to figure out how we can bridge that gap.

How can we help make accounting an attractive profession for the new generation?

How can we reimagine the accounting industry for the general public so that they see us as a valuable asset to their business?

How can we encourage a culture within firms that fosters community and mental and physical well-being without compromising growth?

How can we help accountants find balance in their work and life so they don't feel like leaving the industry is the only option?

I see so many things changing soon—good changes. My business is just a small part of it. Any way that I can make that change would be my privilege.

It would mean that I left a legacy of impact—a life lived more than just for the sake of being here and going through it.

We all leave a legacy, either intentional or unintentional. I want people to think of their businesses from that perspective.

What kind of legacy are you leaving behind?

the brain health revolution

EMPOWERING WOMEN TO TAKE CHARGE OF THEIR BRAIN HEALTH

GENELL LEMLEY

in /genelllemley

renewherwellness.com

Genell Lemley, an Integrated Nutrition health coach and Dr. Amen licensed brain health trainer, helps lead the brain health revolution. Her journey from the corporate world to brain health advocacy began when prioritizing her physical health improved her mental clarity, revealing the profound mind-body connection. Conversations with women about their health concerns, particularly brain health, and witness-ing cognitive decline in her family and friends' families high-lighted the urgent need for advocacy and education.

Genell empowers high-performing women to reach peak cognitive performance and overall well-being. Her approach uses evidence-based brain health strategies, offering per-sonalized coaching that transforms lives.

Drawing from her corporate background, Genell relates to the challenges faced by high-performing women. She guides clients through practical, sustainable lifestyle changes that enhance mental clarity, resilience, and productivity.

Genell's warm, expert coaching creates a supportive envi-ronment where women feel empowered to prioritize their cognitive health. Through her work, she is not just coaching individuals but nurturing a community of women leading the charge in brain health awareness.

How do you define impact?

Impact is more than just what we do or achieve. It is how our actions affect others and shape the world around us, like a ripple in the water spreading out and touching everything it meets. Impact is the mark we leave behind, how we change over time, how we interact, the choices we make, and what we give to others.

I've learned that relationships and experiences shape us and help us understand what is important. Through tough times, I learned invaluable insights into resilience, empathy, self-discovery, and the importance of pushing forward even when things are hard. These experiences made me who I am today, someone who cares deeply about making a difference.

When things don't go as planned, we learn from them and grow. Impact is about the hurdles we overcome *and* the triumphs we celebrate. Life's hurdles teach us valuable lessons along the way, and our impact is how we affect change due to those lessons learned.

My work as a health coach is about helping my clients live better lives. It's about seeing them transform, reach their goals, feel empowered, and know that I have played a part in that. To paraphrase Abraham Lincoln, it *is not about adding years to their lives but life to their years.*

Making an impact is about touching lives, making positive changes, and leaving behind a legacy of kindness and compassion.

Looking back over your life, who has impacted you most, and what specific advice or guidance from them has not only influenced your personal growth but also significantly impacted the direction of your professional career?

Although several wonderful people have influenced my life, no one has impacted me more than my late husband John.

We started as high school sweethearts when I boldly asked him to Sadie Hawkins. Our relationship deepened through the different paths we took, growing together rather than apart in those transformative years.

John was my heart's compass. His parents' legacy inspired his philosophy about life, and that really impacted who I am today. He believed that while grades and achievements were important, they weren't as important as the relationships we nurture and the integrity we bring to our daily lives

He was incredibly open-minded and always sought to understand people and truly see them. For 33 years, John was not just my partner but my rock, my biggest supporter, and my guiding light. He was kind, thoughtful, funny, and consistently led by example, showing deep integrity in both his personal and professional life.

He was passionate and committed to his work of creating affordable housing. Shortly before his cancer diagnosis, he started his own business as an investment banker, working with developers, investors, and municipalities to help orchestrate the development and financing of affordable housing projects in cities nationwide. He was a leader and a beacon of positivity, even when he was diagnosed with a rare type of cancer with a less-than-hopeful prognosis.

John faced life with remarkable positivity. His fight and determination were commendable and inspiring. His resilience in the face of adversity was inspiring, particularly when he participated in fundraising bike rides for cancer research, even under the weight of his own illness.

He transformed his battle into a rallying cry for hope, participating in grueling 100-mile bike rides to raise awareness and funds for cancer research. Each pedal was a testament to his indomitable spirit.

When John died, it wasn't just a personal loss but a transformational moment for me. Witnessing his dedication and impact, I felt a strong desire to find my own meaningful path. It ignited in me a relentless drive to make a tangible difference like he had aspired to.

The corporate world suddenly seemed devoid of meaning, and I knew I needed to seek out my new calling—something with impact and meaning. Although it took me a while to find that direction, it ultimately led me to become a health coach.

Think about the personal challenges you've overcome in your life. How did the obstacles that you've overcome play a part in the impact that you make now?

The five-year season of grief I endured, beginning with John's passing, profoundly shaped my purpose, who I am today and the work I do.

After losing my husband, I also lost both my parents, a lifelong girlfriend, an aunt, my three dogs, and even my job. Each loss compounded the one before, making it feel as if I was being hit with wave after wave of sorrow. I didn't allow myself to process these emotions initially; instead, I kept pushing through life, not realizing the toll it was taking on me internally.

This continual process of enduring and overcoming gave me a deep understanding of pain, loss, and resilience. Although another person's pain may differ, I understand the physical and mental effects of pain and loss.

It wasn't until John had passed that I realized how much I had neglected myself while he was ill. Reflecting on a photo from that time, I saw someone I barely recognized. I hadn't cared for myself, physically or mentally, and it showed. I gained weight, was out of shape, and was exhausted.

It was my wake-up call, and it was a catalyst for my transformation. I joined a gym and changed my diet. As I began prioritizing my physical health, I found my mental clarity improving as well. This personal transformation not only boosted my energy but also brought into sharp focus how interconnected our physical and mental health are.

This transformation eventually led me to become a health coach for high-performing women, specifically focused on brain health. Three main reasons drove my decision to focus on brain health:

First, my experience highlighted the relationship between physical health and mental clarity.

Second, when I talked to other women about their primary health concerns, most mentioned they worried about brain health after watching their own parents' cognitive decline (the statistical reality is that two-thirds of Alzheimer's diagnoses are women).

My family's experiences with cognitive decline underscored the third reason. My parents, my aunt, and my friends' parents suffered some form of cognitive decline, and these personal ties were alarming.

I realized the urgent need for more advocacy and education around the possibility of delaying or preventing cognitive decline. Our fate is not sealed. Proactive measures can significantly strengthen our cognitive abilities at any age.

My approach as a health coach focused on brain health is tailored to high-performing women over 45 who often face immense pressures that can affect their cognitive health. I focus on enhancing cognitive functions through lifestyle changes that improve mental clarity, resilience, and productivity. In doing so, they not only can enhance their personal and professional lives but also take proactive steps toward delaying or preventing dementia and Alzheimer's.

My approach enables women to lead more vibrant, productive, and fulfilling lives, profoundly impacting their personal and professional environments.

With this work, I carry forward John's legacy of impacting others. By turning my personal strategies into a source of strength and inspiration for others, I strive to be the beacon of hope and empowerment John was to me.

This is the impact I am meant to have: a tribute to a life beautifully lived and a love eternally cherished.

———————————

Reflect on a moment in your professional life that you perceived as a failure. How did this experience lead to your most significant lessons of impact? Share how you have applied these lessons to positively influence your life and the lives of others.

Challenging experiences have led to some of the most significant lessons and impactful transformations in my personal and professional journey.

After deciding not to return to the corporate world, I first ventured into real estate and house flipping. I was driven by a passion for real estate and design and a desire to build something successful on my own terms.

Although I experienced some early success, this venture took a discouraging turn when I decided to partner.

My partners experienced some financial troubles, and I carried the financial burden.

Then, a builder overextended himself on multiple projects, and the ripple effect took a toll on my business.

Despite these challenges, I chose not to default on the loans. While I preserved my integrity and ethical standards, this choice led to significant financial loss and left me questioning my judgment and abilities.

The experience was humbling and left me feeling like a failure. This period of my life was filled with self-doubt and fear of making another misstep.

Even now, I occasionally grapple with lingering fears. But hindsight is 20/20, and I did learn some valuable lessons. I learned how to:

Trust Myself: I learned to trust my own judgment and abilities, rather than relying too heavily on the expertise of others.

Develop Resilience and Perseverance: I developed resilience by navigating challenges, which taught me the importance of perseverance even when the path forward was daunting.

See the Connection Between Self-Identity and Failure: I realized that a business failure did not define me. How I handled and overcame challenges said much more about me. I learned to separate my self-worth from my professional setbacks.

Gain Strength from Struggles: I recognized that strength often comes from facing and overcoming difficult situations.

This "failure" profoundly influenced my decision to pivot professionally.

SUCCESS COMES FROM RISING AFTER FALLING AND TRANSFORMING CHALLENGES INTO STEPPING STONES FOR GROWTH.

I decided to pursue a career as a health coach, aiming to help individuals achieve their health and wellness goals with a caring and holistic approach.

Applying these lessons has not only enriched my life but also allowed me to empower others. As a health coach, I emphasize the importance of resilience, self-trust, and the understanding that setbacks are not endpoints but part of a learning journey. This mindset shift is the key.

Success comes from rising after falling and transforming challenges into stepping stones for growth.

How do you ensure your business practices align with ethical and sustainable principles while balancing profitability with making a positive impact?

Continuing to make a positive impact while balancing ethics and profitability involves a combination of strategic client selection and a steadfast commitment to my core values.

My core values focus on four guiding principles:

The first principle is focused on **long-term sustainability.** My specialization in brain health for high-performing women over 45 isn't just a temporary trend but a lasting necessity. The ongoing, increasing need for health and cognitive wellness lends itself to ethical practice by promoting genuine well-being.

Focusing on lifestyle changes that improve cognition and mental clarity and can slow down or prevent cognitive decline allows me to contribute sustainably to the overall health system.

This preventative approach reduces the future burden on healthcare systems and aligns with the broader ethical, social, and ethical goals.

The second principle is **selective clientele**. To grow my business, it's essential that I choose the right clients. Clients who are likely to benefit from my coaching are crucial to the long-term success and sustainability of my business, or any business for that matter.

Being selective with my clientele leads to more satisfying, productive, and profitable relationships in the long run. If I determine a prospective customer isn't the right fit, it's beneficial for both of us, as I certainly don't want any potential client to spend money on something that isn't going to work out.

Focusing on clients who align with my core values signals that I'm not in the business of simply making a profit, but of making a lasting impact. Strategic selection minimizes potential conflicts and enhances the effectiveness of my coaching. Aligned clients are more likely to be receptive to my guidance and committed to the process.

Choosing the correct clientele also benefits my business by maintaining the integrity of my brand and protecting its reputation. Aligned clients attract others who appreciate and seek out my unique value proposition. Being selective with my clientele leads to higher satisfaction with my services and enhanced profitability through loyal client relationships.

The third principle is **ethical pricing and profitability.** My pricing reflects the value I provide, enabling me to operate profitably without compromising ethical standards.

Clients who recognize the value of my specialized service are willing to pay appropriate rates to support a sustainable business model. By being selective, I avoid overextending my resources and diluting the quality of my services.

My fourth principle is **community and impact.** I empower my clients to lead more vibrant and productive lives, benefiting their professional and personal circles. This broader impact highlights the role of ethical business practices in contributing to community well-being.

Each client success story becomes a testament to the effectiveness and integrity of my practice, promoting sustainable business growth through positive word of mouth and client referrals.

This approach not only ensures the longevity and success of my business but also fosters a significant and lasting impact on society.

What role do partnerships and collaborations play in amplifying the impact of your business? How do you identify and cultivate meaningful relationships with other business leaders?

Partnerships and collaborations play a huge role in amplifying my business's impact. They offer opportunities to leverage resources, tap into expertise, and expand networks beyond what I could achieve alone.

Being an entrepreneur can feel lonely and isolating. Without in-person office connections, relationships become even more vital. Fostering meaningful relationships sometimes means stepping out of our comfort zone and engaging with others actively. Whether through mastermind groups, online communities, conferences, or social media, each interaction presents an opportunity to create new connections.

Personally, being part of a mastermind group has been a game-changer for me. Relationships evolve as members collaborate, support, and challenge each other's development. For example, contributing to a colleague's podcast or providing a guest post enriches their content while expanding my reach.

THE BRAIN HEALTH REVOLUTION

Expanding on collaboration opportunities, I am actively exploring affiliate partnerships and joint ventures to align with complementary businesses. By collaborating with a functional medicine practitioner, sleep specialist, or metabolic nutritionist, I can enhance my services as a health coach focused on improving brain health. These partnerships will broaden the scope of support for clients and enrich the overall value proposition, providing comprehensive solutions tailored to individual needs.

By actively cultivating connections and collaborations, I enrich my entrepreneurial journey and contribute to the collective success of my business ecosystem.

Looking ahead, what are your aspirations for the future impact of your business, and how do you plan to continue evolving and innovating in this area?

My aspirations for my business's impact are deeply rooted in broadening my impact and reaching a wider audience to empower ALL women to prioritize their cognitive well-being.

Education and awareness campaigns will remain the cornerstones of my approach. I am passionate about highlighting the significance of brain health to high-performing women over 45. Leveraging platforms like social media, webinars, and workshops can raise awareness about the profound impact of lifestyle choices on cognitive health.

I also aim to provide accessible support to a broader demographic, ensuring we leave no woman behind in their journey toward optimal brain health. Speaking at wellness conferences and corporate events will enhance my visibility and allow me to network with other individuals and organizations who are passionate about advancing women's health.

Eventually, I would like to integrate specialized coaching programs into corporate wellness initiatives and senior housing facilities.

Belonging and camaraderie are great sources of inspiration and motivation for women who prioritize their brain health. Building a supportive community is paramount to fostering lasting change. Creating online forums, support groups, and membership platforms are additional ways I plan to facilitate meaningful connections and peer support among women on their wellness journey.

Lastly, I am committed to continuous professional development. Whether attending conferences or forming partnerships with healthcare and wellness professionals, I'm committed to enhancing the effectiveness of my services and providing the highest standards of care to my clients.

Together, we can reshape the narrative around brain health, inspiring women to prioritize their cognitive well-being and embrace a lifestyle that fosters long-term brain health.

the butterfly effect

TONI BURNS

in /toni-burns-healthbenefits

reimaginebenefits.com

Toni is the Executive Director at Reimagine Benefits, where she leverages her extensive expertise as a licensed health and life insurance agent across over 30 states. Specializing in guiding individuals, families, and small business owners through transitions, she excels in crafting customized private health insurance plans that allow clients to retain their preferred doctors while safeguarding their future well-being.

Before her career in health insurance, Toni made a significant impact in the media industry. While still at the University of Michigan, she began her career at WDIV-TV, the NBC affiliate in Detroit, where she worked as an associate producer and assistant director in both the special projects and news departments. Her passion for advocacy led her to New York City at age 25, where she represented over 26 TV stations as an advertising rep, marking a pivotal shift in her professional journey.

Later, her company promoted her to Houston to serve regional TV stations as their Houston advertising rep. This is where she not only met her husband, but found her passion to help teenagers as a mentor and core leader. Along with a few young adult friends at the church, she helped begin the Life Teen program at her local Houston church. It is still going strong after 27 years.

Most recently, she was a founding board member for the Sugar Land Jewels, a local chapter for the National Charity

League whose motto is *"Mothers and daughters serving their community together"*.

Now, as a health agent and health advocate, she continues to impact individuals and families by providing "peace of mind" through health insurance so when those unexpected moments happen, they have protection.

Toni lives in Sugar Land, Texas with her husband, Mark, and has three children, Brendon, Ashley and Kaitlyn that are attending undergraduate and graduate colleges as they venture out into the world sharing their "butterfly effect".

How do you define impact?

Impact is making a positive change to help someone see their inner opportunities and providing a resource and an avenue to help empower and elevate either the situation, the community, or that person to live a better path and leave something better behind.

It's the past and future intertwined. The more that we can help impact our communities, leaders, and children, the more we can all spread our light and help others become the best that they can be and change the world together.

Looking back over your life, who has impacted you most, and what specific advice or guidance from them has not only influenced your personal growth but also significantly impacted the direction of your professional career?

I've had a lot of amazing people in my life, not just one person, but a whole community of people that I'm blessed to have in my life.

I remember my dad saying, "Always try to make a hundred thousand dollars so that you don't have to depend on anybody, but you can also pay it forward."

I always keep that in the back of my heart. He was a man of few words, but that was the one thing that stuck with me.

I am blessed to have a family that inspires and supports me. My mother, sisters, cousins, and aunts have also provided me with female support throughout my life, encouraging me to try new things and find my authentic self.

Most people think of the impact of a leader or someone they've worked with as providing the largest impact, but my friends from middle school are a core group that had a great impact on me.

I was fortunate to find myself in a group of friends who consistently empowered me. At a time when I struggled with a positive self-image, they encouraged me to pursue cheerleading, recognizing my natural inclination to support and uplift others. Their belief in me helped me embrace my "servant's heart" and step into a role I would have never considered on my own. This newfound confidence fueled me through high school and college, instilling an unstoppable mindset that has continued to drive me forward.

Looking back, choosing the right friends in your inner circle is very important. That decision can impact which path you choose, whether it's in high school, college, or business.

Think about the personal challenges you've overcome in your life. How did the obstacles that you've overcome play a part in the impact that you make now?

When COVID-19 hit, it felt as if the whole world had come to a standstill. I had just transitioned from a stable job in 2019 to start my own business, leveraging my expertise in business and marketing to support small businesses and entrepreneurs. But with the pandemic reshaping every aspect of life, I faced an unexpected challenge: many businesses were closing, advertising budgets were slashed, and the need for my services dwindled.

As the world grappled with these changes, I faced the daunting reality of financial uncertainty. I had invested my resources into my new venture, leaving behind a secure job and a stable income. With my older son returning home from college and our family of five all living together again, the pressure to find a new path was immense.

In the midst of this upheaval, I realized that my calling was shifting. I felt a profound shift in purpose— moving from marketing to directly helping people in need. This period of challenge forced me to reimagine my career and seek out a path that could sustain my family and contribute meaningfully during these uncertain times. Adapting to this new direction not only helped me navigate the financial strains but also allowed me to make a tangible impact by supporting others through their own difficulties.

How was I still going to make that impact? In 2020, I chose to pivot and reimagine myself. I created a new company, *"Reimagine Benefits"* to impact others, help people through the confusion in that space and be their health agent and advocate. And I'm loving it! It has taken off, too. When you serve people with a servant's heart and solve their needs, great things can happen together.

Several years ago, I faced a major surgery and found myself without an advocate to guide me through the complex maze of preparation, doctor timelines, and health insurance. I was uncertain whether the guidance I was receiving was truly in my best interest or if my health insurance would adequately cover the costs. This experience highlighted the importance of having someone who could navigate these challenges effectively.

Now, as a health insurance agent, I strive to offer that crucial support to others. My goal is to create customized health plans that not only include access to their preferred doctors but also ensure coverage where it's most needed, based on individual needs. I provide guidance to help clients maximize their benefits, aiming to prevent situations where unexpected medical expenses could lead to financial strain.

I've seen firsthand the difference this advocacy can make. For instance, in 2020, I assisted a family who needed to switch their insurance plan after facing rising costs. Just seven months later, the wife was diagnosed with breast cancer and required a double mastectomy. Thanks to the new plan I helped them select, which included critical illness and hospital indemnity benefits, she received financial support to cover her hospital stay and additional expenses..

This experience reinforced my commitment to ensuring that clients have the protection they need, even when they feel healthy. Accidents and illnesses can strike unexpectedly, and having the right insurance plan in place beforehand can make all the difference in navigating these challenging times without the fear of financial devastation.

Another instance that stands out is when a family who had been on their health plan for over 18 months faced an unexpected challenge: their older son broke his leg. Thanks to the plan we had set up, we were able to facilitate reimbursement for his x-rays and surgeries, and his out-of-pocket expenses were reduced to just $500.

Last year, a client, who is an ER doctor, reached out to me at 10:30 PM when her son suffered a double fracture at a sports lesson. While they waited at an ER far from her workplace, her frustration grew as her son's pain worsened. I guided her to an urgent care center nearby for immediate care and arranged for him to receive surgery at her own hospital a few days later. By helping her navigate the situation and find an in-network facility, I ensured her son received timely treatment while keeping costs manageable. Having the right coverage and the right health agent can make an impact and a difference in an individual, family, or business owner.

Reflect on a moment in your professional life that you perceived as a failure. How did this experience lead to your most significant lessons of impact? Share how you have applied these lessons to positively influence your life and the lives of others.

I was once the National Sales Manager for Fox in Houston, overseeing sales reps across half the country, while also juggling the demands of raising three young children. My ultimate ambition was to become a General Manager at a television station, a goal fueled by my passion for working in every department and thriving in the industry.

I vividly recall a moment on a work trip to California, where I was enjoying a top-tier experience at the American Idol semifinals with clients. Despite my professional success, my husband, overwhelmed by managing our family alone, called me that night. The conversation shifted from my exciting day to a crucial discussion about my need to be more present at home. Upon returning, I made the difficult decision to step down from my managerial role and focus solely on being a salesperson.

Little did I know, this shift would align perfectly with a new opportunity to make a significant impact. In July 2005, the Houston Astros were making headlines with a remarkable season, and Fox would be broadcasting the World Series. Drawing on my previous experience at WDIV/NBC and my deep understanding of production, advertising,

> I'VE COME TO REALIZE THAT THERE'S A REASON GOD GUIDES US ALONG CERTAIN PATHS.

and logistics, I proposed creating a local pregame show. This idea, "Road to the Ring," aimed to benefit our advertisers, KRIV/FOX TV station, and the community.

The show was a success and has continued to be a staple during Astros' postseason runs. It not only showcases local businesses but also fosters a vibrant community spirit, demonstrating how shifting my role allowed me to leverage my skills in a new, impactful way.

I've come to realize that there's a reason God guides us along certain paths. During that challenging transition, I was initially distressed about returning to a salesperson role, feeling it was a step back from my management aspirations. Yet, this new path allowed me to make a meaningful impact, whether by supporting local advertisers or enhancing our connection with the community through sports.

Creating the "Road to the Ring" show not only benefited our station and advertisers but also brought a fresh approach to sports programming. It's been rewarding to see this initiative ripple out, with other TV stations adopting similar ideas. Witnessing these small ripples grow into a broader influence has been a gratifying reminder that sometimes the unexpected paths can lead to the most fulfilling impacts.

———

How do you ensure your business practices align with ethical and sustainable principles while balancing profitability with making a positive impact?

My choices have always been guided by my faith and a commitment to doing what's right. While many decisions are driven by financial considerations, I firmly believe that God provides for those who strive to help others. This principle influenced my decision-making even when selecting a franchise.

After leaving KRIV/FOX, my husband and I spent 11 years as franchisees.   We chose a pizza franchise known for its high-quality ingredients and commitment to freshness. Our goal was to make a positive impact on our community, not only through the quality of our product but also by supporting our employees—helping drivers manage debt and improve their financial stability.

When transitioning to health insurance, my focus was on ensuring I could offer a meaningful service. I wanted to be part of a process where I could take the time to educate clients, helping them understand their options and benefits thoroughly, rather than just processing transactions.

Being aligned with the right people, communities, and companies is crucial to me because our time here on Earth is limited. I strive to ensure that my efforts contribute to creating better opportunities and making a positive impact on both the companies I represent and the clients I serve.

———

What role do partnerships and collaborations play in amplifying the impact of your business? How do you identify and cultivate meaningful relationships with other business leaders?

Many people believe that health insurance is a solitary field with little room for collaboration or referral partnerships, but I've found that the opposite is true. I thrive on networking and bringing people together, leveraging my passion for collaboration to enhance the service I provide. My background in team sports has instilled in me a strong appreciation for teamwork and networking, skills I now apply in health insurance.

I take great joy in discovering and fostering communities. With my licensing in 30 states, I actively seek out individuals and professionals who can enrich my network, helping to serve customers more effectively in various regions. By building these connections, I create valuable resources for clients and strengthen the support available within each community.

I aim to be the resource people need and to connect with them.

I'm someone who will be there in the short term and long term, not just to sell them a plan.

That has also helped me get more referrals back. You just never know when that's going to pay off. Everyone passes through our lives at different times, but that intersection is there for a reason. Seeing and acknowledging them and developing them can help create referral partners and collaborations.

There was a time when I would get nervous talking about money or helping others. There's a time in everybody's life when they want to hoard what they make or are so excited about what they've accomplished. I personally would get anxious and feel guilty though from my success. So, I find it's better to give.

I learned to stay still, listen, and make connections. I believe in people's inner and outer circle and beyond. That also creates a ripple effect. I love that impact because you can add to it.

It's like a butterfly that just keeps changing.

We are not meant to stay still, but to evolve and grow.

When you communicate with a positive and energetic vibe, you naturally attract similar energy and people who resonate with that spirit. By sharing your gifts and making a positive impact, you create an environment where others are drawn to collaborate and contribute. This synergy fosters organic partnerships and mutual support, as people are inspired to join forces and share their own resources, creating a dynamic and thriving network.

Looking ahead, what are your aspirations for the future impact of your business, and how do you plan to continue evolving and innovating in this area?

Currently, I'm focused on reaching out to individuals interested in becoming health agents, sharing my approach, methodologies, and the opportunities available in this field. I often ask people whether they are truly fulfilled in their current roles and if they feel they are making a meaningful impact.

My aim is to transfer my passion and energy to others, showing them how to make a difference as health agents and advocates. Just as I did with my pizza franchise, where my goal was to help others thrive and achieve their best, my mission remains centered on empowering individuals to reach their full potential and make a positive impact on the lives of those they serve.

Some people will come into my life for **a reason, a season, or a lifetime**. If I can help them or provide them that faith or strength to become their better self in another job, that's okay, too. Ultimately, I want to inspire and empower people to be a servant to others as they become their best selves.

"AS ONE PERSON I CANNOT CHANGE THE WORLD, BUT I CAN CHANGE THE WORLD OF ONE PERSON."

Paul Shane Spear

the power of a village to inspire an authentic transformation

MARISSA GREEN

in /marissa-green-reimagine-ambition

reimagineambition.co

Climbing ladders used to be Marissa's day job, but healing the hustle for other mothers became her calling.

After climbing ladders at top PR Firms and leading bio-pharma companies, Marissa burnt out as a new mother trying to keep pace with hustle culture and "having it all." All that hard work landed her in the ER with debilitating head-aches, caused by stress. But she walked out of the hospital with the clarity she needed to say, "Enough is enough." She began searching for a different way to parent, work, and thrive—without sacrificing herself or her family.

Inspired by other women taking chances and boldly choosing to do "working motherhood" differently, Marissa began to design work and life on her own terms. She quit her corporate role and started the slow journey of stepping out of the hustle by building a thriving employee experience consulting business. She quickly exceeded her corporate salary, while taking the summers off and slowing down more and more each day.

In honor of the village of women who sparked a new way of thinking inside her, Marissa launched Reimagine Ambition and is on a mission to create a modern-day village for over-worked moms. The village will provide overworked moms with access to the inspiration, support, and tools they need to get off the hamster wheel and start defining work, life, and motherhood on their own terms.

How do you define impact?

Here's what I love about impact: every single person has their own unique ability to deliver impact. How you do it is different from how I do it—but all of it matters.

For many years, I thought the value of my impact was measured by what other people thought of me, or expected me to do. And I aimed to please. I struggled to find a true sense of purpose because I was too caught up in checking someone else's box and trying to deliver value through productivity...

...until I realized that doing great work isn't the end goal.

Sure, it's an important foundation—but it's only part of the equation for meaningful IMPACT.

I found that when I focused on creating a positive transformation for someone or something else— that's when my impact became meaningful. When I was no longer trying to be nice and deliver what people expected. When I created a safe space and the roadmap for a mom, a leader, or a business to step out of what is comfortable. That is when true transformation happens. Because transformation isn't about playing it safe, or comfortable. It's about being willing to step outside those comfortable boundaries and into what you really want.

So, I started using my unique way of seeing the world to transform businesses and lives for the better. And I've never looked back. Today, whether it's my consulting work, coaching overworked moms, or teaching my kids something new, I focus on creating space for positive transformation.

———————

Looking back over your life, who has impacted you most, and what specific advice or guidance from them has not only influenced your personal growth but also significantly impacted the direction of your professional career?

I am the youngest of six kids AND 15 years younger than my closest sibling. As a farming family raised in the Midwest, hard work and entrepreneurial spirit were a way of life for us all. I grew up in awe of my parents, who worked night and day to ensure we had more than they did. And I took notes as each of my siblings found their own version of success in unique and different ways.

Growing up with siblings who were adults meant I had to get really good at curating a village of friends wherever I went—and it has had a profound impact on my life. Eventually, I chose to climb the corporate ladder and move from city to city, growing my village along the way.

TAKE INSPIRATION FROM OTHERS, AND THEN PAVE YOUR OWN PATH.

So, when I tried to pinpoint one person who has impacted me the most, I realized it's not just one person.

I have watched closely—studied even—as my family, friends, colleagues, and mentors worked through challenges and reached new heights. My big takeaway from that study is that everyone tackles life in different ways. This has taught me an important life lesson that I will carry with me forever.

Take inspiration from others, and then pave your own path.

I've started to realize and fully understand (here at the ripe old age of 42) that the happiest people—and thereby the most successful, in my book—are those willing to unapologetically create an authentic path of their own.

All too often, we are pulled to follow the people around us, yet we are most impactful when we live life as our full, authentic selves.

That is what I have learned from the myriad of people around me—influencing me, inspiring me. They all make different choices, believe in different things, and live life in different ways. They helped me see that there are a multitude of possibilities available to me—to all of us. We don't have to follow one path or one way.

We get to make our own.

As a working mom, this collective influence has also shaped the way I design my work/life. After being told by many people that there is only "one way" to be a working mom—and that's to burn out—I have now learned that there are actually millions of ways to follow our dreams without sacrificing ourselves or our families—we just have to find the one that is right for us and be willing to live into it fully.

That's why I'm so passionate about creating a village to inspire other moms with examples of women doing things differently and paving their own way. There is no right way to be a "mother." You can work in the home, outside the home, part-time, or full-time. It's up to you to take influence from the people that most inspire you—and then define a path that is uniquely yours.

———

Reflect on a moment in your professional life that you perceived as a failure. How did this experience lead to your most significant lessons of impact? Share how you have applied these lessons to positively influence your life and the lives of others.

In my last "regular full-time role" (as I like to call it), I had been working toward a promotion. Over the years, titles came to mean everything to me. I poured all of myself into achieving each role by taking on more responsibility (without more pay, or more support) and burning the candle at both ends to ensure nothing fell through the cracks.

I was proud of the impact I was having through my work. I felt like I was growing as a person and was regularly told that I was significantly contributing to the organization. But damn, I wanted that promotion. I thought it would make me feel valued. Really, I wanted it for validation that all my hard work was "worth it."

But it never came. At every review, I'd hear, "One more year," or "You need a bit more time,"... "Just keep going." They kept dangling the carrot and moving the goalpost. Every year, the only thing I seemed to receive—was feeling more and more burnt out.

After giving my everything to my work during the pandemic, I was expecting 2021 to be my year to finally get the promotion. I remember sitting down with my boss at the time, excited and ready to celebrate, when I heard them say, "I think you've got about 12 to 18 more months." My stomach dropped, and it was all I could do to hold it together and politely reply, "I see your point of view and disagree. We'll talk about this another time."

I had to take the time to fully process this blow, but I knew as I walked away at that moment, my perspective on achievement, ambition, and true impact had completely changed. I walked away knowing I needed to redefine what it meant to have a purposeful career as a mother.

The real undercurrent to that story is that as I poured more and more of myself into my career, on a quest to climb the ladder, I continued to feel a distance from my children and myself. This distance grew mile by mile, often unnoticed, until suddenly, I was oceans away from where I wanted to be, and without the one thing that I thought would make it all seem worth it.

For me, NOT receiving that promotion unlocked the realization and understanding of how rooted in achievement I had become—how rooted in achievement society tells us we should be. That fateful conversation also freed me from feeling like I needed to stay on that achievement-driven path. It helped me realize that what I had been doing wasn't working, and it became the catalyst for me to do something different.

All of a sudden, it clicked for me. I finally understood the penalty that so many mothers receive when they have children inside corporate environments. We are seen differently—and in many cases, we even see ourselves differently. Not because we are less capable, or because we can't do the job, but because we all know that we are juggling a second full-time job outside the workplace. And so we work overtime. We double down. We take on more. We suffer quietly. Hoping that no one will notice that it's all too much. Hoping that we can come out on top if we just... keep... hustling.

This realization sparked a fire in me to find a way out

of the hustle and into a life that allows me to follow my dreams, without ending up oceans away from my true purpose and my family.

Since then, I've been on a mission to inspire other overworked moms to reimagine ambition and get the support (and village) they need to chase their dreams without sacrificing themselves.

How do you ensure your business practices align with ethical and sustainable principles while balancing profitability with making a positive impact?

The majority of my consulting work is in pioneering purpose transformation by helping businesses grow through social impact. The entire essence of that work is to help Fortune 500 organizations learn how to do well AND do good by balancing profitability and growth with delivering a positive impact.

That work has changed the way I see business and the way I interpret our responsibilities as business owners and entrepreneurs. I believe I have a responsibility to aim for sustainability, inclusion, and a net-positive impact through my work and my business. For me, it has all been about building the foundations of my business in a way that enables that.

I'm not going to pretend that it's easy, or that I get it right all the time. I'm constantly learning how to do it better, or where I can make a more positive impact. Sustainable practices are more expensive. Driving for inclusion is harder. But all of it is so necessary and important, and the research shows that when you build and deliver your business sustainably, you attract great people and achieve better results, even if they don't always come as fast.

The same goes for a value we hold strong in my consulting work and with Reimagine Ambition—family-first flexibility. I'm here to build a business in balance, and I want that for my team too. When I work in balance with my life and my family, things don't happen as fast as they would if I was all-out 60 hours a week, staying up until midnight to get everything done. That's just a fact.

But our IMPACT is better when we slow down to recharge and find space to do the work in alignment with our values.

The end result for everyone is greater.

What role do partnerships and collaborations play in amplifying the impact of your business? How do you identify and cultivate meaningful relationships with other business leaders?

Partnerships have become a critical foundation of our Reimagine Ambition business strategy, built on the principle of "It takes a village." I realize I don't have to be the only one helping our members transform their lives—it isn't about me—it's about WE. The Reimagine Ambition is the curator and connector, helping overworked moms find a village, the support and the tools they need. And partnerships are the way we are doing it.

Specifically, we use our networks, masterminds, connections made through our podcast, and the simple work of building relationships as tools to cultivate opportunities for collaboration.

I don't see partnerships as transactional exchanges, though. I see partnerships as relationships. They're a mutual connection: I bring someone into my business or ask them to support my community somehow, and then I also ask how I can support them or their community. It's not transactional but an exchange of support. Building relationships, for example, through masterminds and other group collectives, is more about having a collective of support than about networking.

When looking for a team and partners who I want to collaborate with, I try to stretch myself and find people who won't echo my point of view. I always try to get in rooms where it doesn't make immediate sense to me why I'm there. I might not be as far along as they are, or maybe they're a group of people with a completely different business model or perspective. It forces me to challenge myself and ask, "Do I feel **UNcomfortable** enough in this space? Will this group push me to make my work better in ways that I wouldn't have thought of?" It's important to listen to what they have to say, learn from it, and act on it. **If you feel too comfortable, it's time to find a new group that stretches you a little more.**

One of the biggest benefits of becoming an entrepreneur is the greater opportunity to find the right partners and to build amazing business friends who will support you on your journey.

In this world, you have to have people in your corner to tell you to keep going when it gets hard. I need somebody to say, "Don't give up; keep going. It's hard, but you can do it." That's honestly been the biggest and most unexpected impact of these relationships for me.

Looking ahead, what are your aspirations for the future impact of your business, and how do you plan to continue evolving and innovating in this area?

We are launching the Reimagine Ambition village later this year. Right now, we are in the discovery phase, working with different moms and individuals to provide input into what they want that village to be.

We are on a mission to serve a million women through this village. I want this to be a space where overworked moms can come together to heal from the hustle that makes us feel overworked, and craft a new way to live, work, and parent, without sacrificing ourselves.

Innovation is a critical part of how we are bringing this village to life. We are driven to curate innovative and meaningful experiences that reach moms and engage them in a conversation—without taking too much of their time or capacity. I know this is especially important for overworked moms on the brink of burnout—particularly if they're in a corporate environment. They won't show up for the "usual" stuff. I want to create the space that they will show up for, which means we have to do it completely differently.

We need to develop something that doesn't exist yet, so we're constantly innovating. My consulting work relies on a method called, human-centered design, to create products and strategies that put the target audience at the center of the design. We're doing the same with our village. It's all about putting overworked moms at the center and designing around them. We have to see them first for them to feel seen. We have to hear them first for them to feel heard.

My experience is not the same as every other woman's. That is why the village and collective community influence is so important. Each of us has our own experiences that shaped us, and that will shape the decisions we'll make for our futures. I'm trying to find connective experiences where moms can feel safe enough to slow down, heal the hustle, and get back to living a life that they love.

The answer to that will look different for every member, but I'm confident we can create a community where women can be supported in the choices that work best for them.

cultivating a legacy of aligned values

LISA MORRIS

in /lisa-j-morris-shrm-cp-mba

Lisa Morris is a dynamic success coach dedicated to empowering women to transform their bank accounts, careers, and lives. Lisa is not just a coach but also a guide, strategist, and advisor. With a deep understanding of financial struggles and personal resilience, she guides women on a path to financial independence and fulfillment. She believes every woman deserves the life, freedom, and joy they envision.

For many years, Lisa was a broke single mom juggling 2 to 3 jobs at a time, living paycheck to paycheck, and facing the daunting burden of over a million dollars in debt. Despite these challenges, she refused to let her circumstances define her future. Through sheer determination, strategic financial planning, a money mindset shift, and a relentless pursuit of her goals, she paid off her debt and built a life of abundance and freedom. Today, she not only enjoys financial stability but also has her money working for her, and she travels the world exploring new cultures and sharing her journey with others.

Lisa helps women build lives of financial and time freedom, enabling them to create sustainable wealth while enjoying the flexibility to pursue their passions. She empowers busy, dynamic professional women to design, plan, and live their dream lives from inception to all-out through the success method.

How do you define impact?

Impact is helping, educating, and following with a heart center in everything you do. Impact can be the littlest thing towards somebody, or it can be life-changing. But if you continuously walk through life thinking, *"How can I add value to somebody?"* then you're always impacting.

Looking back over your life, who has impacted you most, and what specific advice or guidance from them has not only influenced your personal growth but also significantly impacted the direction of your professional career?

While I was growing up, there was a woman who came to mind. I don't remember her name, but she was the person who first said, "Hey, I think you have dyslexia," and nobody knew what it was at the time. She changed the direction of my education entirely and greatly impacted me.

A second person would be my high school English teacher, Alice Root, also known as Miss Root. She helped me with my grammar, spelling, etc., all the way through college, so that was very impactful to me.

As I moved into my career, I've encountered many people who have impacted me, but some people stand out the most.

One is Melanie Greenough, who helped me pay off millions of dollars in debt and taught me many skills that I now teach other people in my coaching career.

And a woman named Nancy Ganote had faith in me that I could make a hundred thousand dollars in one year. Which sounded crazy to me at the time, but now I make that and more! And her confidence in me, her "knowing" I could do it, really allowed me to go out and do it. She instilled that sense of self-respect and drive in me.

Think about the personal challenges you've overcome in your life. How did the obstacles that you've overcome play a part in the impact that you make now?

These obstacles are such a strong part of my story and my impact in teaching women how to overcome things and how to get where they want to go no matter what's in front of them. It's not the circumstance that's in front of you. It's how you address that circumstance.

My dyslexia has taught me motivation, strength, and the ability to overcome anything that comes my way. My dyslexia will never go away; it's always going to be a part of me. I can't take medication to get rid of it. It's always going to be there. That has taught me how to overcome an obstacle that will never go away.

I was divorced and a single mom at a very young age. When I was 29 years old, I had a baby at home, my son was one year old at the time, and my husband of seven years walked out on us. Shortly after that, I was laid off because the economy went bonkers on us, and I couldn't find a job.

I quickly learned what it means to be "overqualified."

My dad used to say that all the time. He'd come home from a job interview and say, "They tell me I'm overqualified." And as a child, I thought, "What's overqualified? How can that be bad?"

But I found out what that was. Doing all the things they tell us to do—get a degree (I had all the way to an MBA) and land a professional job. It was for the birds! I could get a job. In 2008, I was laid off as an Area Human Resource Manager for an airline catering company. I could not find a job. After getting hired at the Kentucky Department of Correction as a Correctional Officer, one of the interviewers in my interview told me, "They did not want to hire you because you were overqualified. I knew your work ethic, I fought for you." The feeling that went through my heart when I heard this was so scary and depressing.

I then took it upon myself to learn how to prepare for situations throughout my life that could affect my income. I started learning how to prepare for circumstances that would affect my family. Partnering with mentors and coaches was a huge part of that.

These obstacles are such a strong part of my story and my impact in teaching women how to overcome things and how to get where they want to go no matter what's in front of them. It's not the circumstance that's in front of you. It's how you address that circumstance.

Reflect on a moment in your professional life that you perceived as a failure. How did this experience lead to your most significant lessons of impact? Share how you have applied these lessons to positively influence your life and the lives of others.

When I was laid off and was living on government assistance with my 2 boys, it felt like rock bottom. That led me to depression and anxiety and all those labels that they put on you when you're in those situations. I felt like I was a failure in my profession.

But really, God was setting me up for something better. The universe was setting me up for something better. I was first employed at Walmart as an associate and worked at Cracker Barrel as a waitress. Later, it was during my time as a Correctional Officer that I met my husband, my lifelong sweetheart, and my best friend.

It's funny because I look back on that. I was in such a bad place emotionally, yet it was one of the most cherished moments in my life. I wouldn't be where I am today if that had never happened. I wouldn't be coaching women on how to get out of debt, how to have multiple sources of income, and how to set their lives up for success. If I hadn't endured that situation, where I felt like a total failure, who couldn't keep a roof over my kid's head, food on the table, and all that stuff, it turned out my personal lifelong lesson has ended up impacting many other women over the last 10 years. It's crazy!

———————

How do you ensure your business practices align with ethical and sustainable principles while balancing profitability with making a positive impact?

I only live by ethical and moral principles. I think you have to live by your personal values. When you're misaligned with those values, those ethics, then you're not going to feel good inside, no matter what. I just walk through life that way.

I really teach the women that I work with how to live in alignment with their personal ethics and beliefs, whether they are small business owners themselves or they work in a corporate environment. You have to live in your values.

I also teach it to young families. I teach them to come together and write values down as a group. I even teach them to post them on the walls of their house so that when, for example, their child lies to them, they can come back to that value that's posted on the wall and say, "We walk in the value of trust, and you're not telling the truth, and that makes me not trust you."

I didn't do it when my kids were little, but I wish I would have.

Recently, I talked with a woman who is a plant manager, and she's having some problems at her plant. I asked her whether she was relating their company policies back to the company's core values.

She didn't understand.

I told her the importance of "buy-in" for employee satisfaction. You can get the employees to buy into the company values by having them help you write them and making it a group effort everyone can be proud of.

What role do partnerships and collaborations play in amplifying the impact of your business? How do you identify and cultivate meaningful relationships with other business leaders?

Because I'm an introverted extrovert, I can come out of my shell when I'm talking one-on-one with people, but I get really nervous if I have to talk in front of a lot of people.

COLLABORATION HAS TAKEN MY CORPORATE CAREER AND MY BUSINESS TO AMAZING LEVELS.

I truly believe in collaboration. Collaboration has taken my corporate career and my business to amazing levels. It allows me to add value to others by helping them solve their problems. And the people I collaborate with have returned value to me as well. I am currently collaborating with a banking professional to bring a women's group to our local community. This collaboration between a group of women is bringing blessings—networks, opportunities, support—to other professional women.

For introverts like me, I teach them to use an acronym called **FORM** when they meet and talk with new people.

Family, **O**ccupation, **R**elationships, and **M**essage.

Relying on the FORM method of starting conversations has really amplified my life in a lot of ways. The first three topics are things people can easily relate to and understand. "Message" might be you selling something, educating somebody on what you do, or whatever is relevant to the situation. I've used that all my life, and now I never feel like people are strangers.

Looking ahead, what are your aspirations for the future impact of your business, and how do you plan to continue evolving and innovating in this area?

I want to leave a legacy for my boys and the values we hold in our family. Everything that I teach about values and ethics in my business is either something I learned from raising a family or something I learned in a professional setting and was able to later teach my boys.

Outside my personal legacy for my family, I want to leave that value with every person I see. I want to amplify another person's value which will, in turn, amplify somebody else's value and somebody else's value, when you start lifting people up, it just keeps multiplying. I always try to be encouraging to people when I meet with them, and I give them a nugget to go forward with. I always want to encourage them to take that nugget and teach somebody else.

My ultimate, quantifiable goal is to help a thousand women become happier, healthier, and wealthier over the next 2 years.

move well, eat well, live well

DR. ANJALI AGRAWAL

in /dranjalidc

backinbalancehealth.com

Dr. Anjali Agrawal, founder of Back In Balance, is a non-popping, non-cracking chiropractor and integrative functional nutrition specialist. With nearly 20 years of running a thriving practice and 15 years collaborating with corporate workplaces, she empowers individuals worldwide to restore their health and vitality. Dr. Anjali is passionate about helping families achieve symptom-free living and enhancing the health of future generations through a holistic approach to moving well, eating well, and living well.

Residing in the Bay Area, California, with her husband and two young daughters, Dr. Anjali's own parenting journey has deepened her commitment to guiding families toward better health decisions at every stage. She firmly believes that each person is unique, and their care should be tailored to meet their individual needs. Dr. Anjali is dedicated to unlocking the full potential of the body by providing the personalized support it requires to thrive.

———————

How do you define impact?

To me, impact is what causes people to change their actions or behaviors based on new information they receive, thereby altering the entire course of their future.

———————

Looking back over your life, who has impacted you most, and what specific advice or guidance from them has not only influenced your personal growth but also significantly impacted the direction of your professional career?

There are countless people who have impacted my life in so many different ways, but I'll start with my mom. My mom was a stay-at-home mom who took care of all the household tasks while raising my younger brother and me. This allowed my dad to focus on work and provide for us as the breadwinner.

Growing up, I am grateful that all of us were pretty healthy. In the event that I was coming down with a cold or anything of the sort, my mom would have some kind of home remedy for me to take, and they were pretty much all I needed. From a very young age, I watched her be very mindful about giving us nutritious foods, leading by example, and taking the time and effort to make freshly cooked food daily for our family. Additionally, we would spend every summer visiting extended family in India, where we would visit the local homeopath for any health needs. Even into early adulthood, I didn't actually know who my general physician was, as I hadn't ever met them!

While my dad was also generally healthy, he dealt with mental stress in a very different way than how my mom navigated stress. He would sometimes need some over-the-counter medications to help manage his tension headaches or to be able to get restful sleep. In watching his experience, I began to unknowingly develop a stronger sense of seeing the silver lining of various situations, helping me to manage my (albeit fairly minimal at the time) mental stress with more ease.

While it didn't involve a particular person, I decided to spend my four years of high school volunteering at a prominent local hospital. After working in a variety of departments, however, I became a little bit panicked—while I was glad that my time at the hospital brought new patient faces each week (meaning nobody was there for long), I was still very interested in pursuing a career in *health* care which allowed for an opportunity to get to know my patients beyond their symptoms and go beyond the urgent quick fix of medications and/or surgery.

So that's where my first actual boss, Dr. Wells, came into my life and introduced me to this whole new world of chiropractic. Prior to meeting her, I truly had no idea that chiropractors were involved in health care in any capacity! After spending a short time working in two chiropractic offices that summer, I was amazed that there was a profession that looked at the whole person, and strived to identify the root cause of symptoms. (Side note—my dad also started receiving adjustments, and finally had a way to regulate his nervous system and alleviate his tension headaches without medication!)

Years later, when I first started in practice as an associate, I was working in a practice where my boss was integrating chiropractic care along with functional medicine, and she was working with families to support their perinatal and postpartum journey in a more holistic way. I was elated! While attending chiropractic school, I was very interested in specializing in perinatal/pediatric care and also in nutrition. However, my mental and time bandwidth left me feeling like I had to choose. So I decided to choose the former. Once I started in practice, I got to see the integration of chiropractic and nutrition, or structure and function, on a daily basis, which was incredible. When we transitioned ownership a few months later, I did a deep dive into functional nutrition to effectively continue to care for the existing practice members and support new families coming in for care. Having had the opportunity to see the clinical application of functional nutrition in a chiropractic practice the prior six months made the transition of becoming a new practice owner significantly more manageable, though!

I am so grateful for all the mentors, teachers, and people who have imparted various lessons and invaluable advice along the way. I am always learning something new, whether from my husband or kids, practice members, or even in seemingly small interactions each day.

Think about the personal challenges you've overcome in your life. How did the obstacles that you've overcome play a part in the impact that you make now?

I think the biggest realization was recognizing that you don't have to follow one specific path. The first major experience for me was when I was transitioning from the idea of pursuing a career in chiropractic instead of medicine. I came to appreciate that there are numerous ways to be in healthcare without necessarily following the more traditional trajectory of attending med school. I was choosing the road less traveled, and that led to a lot of questions from friends and family. While their intentions were good, I had to get stronger in my conviction to pursue this unfamiliar track.

Once I entered chiropractic school, I again saw that there are many ways to practice chiropractic, run a practice, and help the community that you're in. There are more than 100 chiropractic techniques, and we really only learned less than a handful in school.

Did I want to work with kids, adjust extremities or spine only, focus on nutrition, specialize in sports chiropractic, offer perinatal care, study chiropractic neurology, emphasize radiology, and geriatrics, or have a general practice?

Did I want to see patients every 5 minutes, 15 minutes, 20–30 minutes, or every hour?

Did I want an open adjusting area with multiple tables or a private room where I could see one person or family at a time?

Did I want to accept insurance or be out-of-network?

There were chiropractors who had found success in various models, but I had to determine what

I HAD TO DETERMINE WHAT BROUGHT ME JOY AND HOW I COULD BEST SERVE MY PRACTICE MEMBERS.

brought me joy and how I could best serve my practice members.

While I was in school, I was part of a group of students who were self-proclaimed "audible junkies," meaning that we didn't believe the adjustment took place unless we heard it (despite being taught that it was about movement, not the sound). Within my first year of practice, however, more and more people started coming in to see me who were requesting that I not perform any manual adjustments on their necks. As a result, I had to adapt and started performing more low-force or non-force adjustments. Surprisingly, I began noticing that people could hold their adjustments for longer periods of time as compared to when they were receiving manual adjustments!

Ultimately, it was the understanding that there really isn't a cookie-cutter template for success or anything we are trying to achieve. We are all unique, with our own experiences, ideas, thoughts, beliefs, etc. This means that we can only create change and impact by recognizing how to personalize the templates we have available and adapting them accordingly.

It is my goal to help educate and guide families to make the small shifts that will have the greatest impact on them. It is about modifying/changing a lifestyle—not a quick and temporary fix, so it has to be realistic and sustainable. This gives people an opportunity to explore ideas that may be different from the most common path, or perhaps at least take different action than what they may have previously considered.

How do you ensure your business practices align with ethical and sustainable principles while balancing profitability with making a positive impact?

I want to walk the walk and talk the talk. If I'm not doing it myself, I don't want to recommend it to people. Because I worked on improving my hydration several years back, it's something that I can talk about with my practice members. I have much more conviction and confidence because I see the difference. Then, I'm not just giving recommendations for things I don't actually believe in or things I won't do for myself or my family.

In my practice, I often say, "There's ideal, and then there's reality. I'm here to help make your reality more ideal." Nothing is necessarily good or bad, so it just depends on how our individual bodies respond. For example, I would typically ask the following:

How do you feel stress impacts you?
How often do you move/stretch?
What do you eat/crave/avoid?
How often do you poop and urinate?
What do you drink daily?
What (if anything) do you put on your skin?
What do you use to clean your home?
What do you do for self-care?

And so many more questions!

If your body is trying to signal that something needs attention and change, how can you ask different questions so that you can make those impactful changes accordingly?

Yes, you may have high blood pressure, but *why* is it high? What is actually happening in the body that is affecting your blood pressure? Do you have a blood pressure medication deficiency? When it comes to urgent care, the medical model is necessary, and I'm so grateful to have access to it.

But when it comes to the day-to-day management of health, too often, we have given up ownership of taking responsibility for our actions.

I constantly keep my "why" and my purpose of empowering people through education at the top of my mind. Whether I'm working with a family 1:1 in my chiropractic practice, doing virtual functional nutrition coaching, or even teaching employees at a corporate office, my primary goal is to help families move well, eat well, and live well by managing their health care differently.

———

What role do partnerships and collaborations play in amplifying the impact of your business? How do you identify and cultivate meaningful relationships with other business leaders?

It's played a huge role in my practice, especially in the past few years. I've had the great blessing of being in different communities where the people who are showing up are in it to build support but also allow a little bit of challenge for growth. It's not criticism, but it's somebody who can say, "That sounds amazing. Have you considered X, Y, and Z?"

The other key aspect of networking and collaborations for me has been to outsource tasks that are outside my zone of genius or excellence to people whose zones of genius are in those tasks! Yes, I could probably figure out the task, but in doing so, I would take a much longer amount of time, it likely wouldn't be as great as a pro, *and* I have made myself less available to share my actual strengths! So ultimately, I'm more lonely working solo, I've spent more time, and I made less money because I was less available to offer only what I could do. The idea of investing in other people's talents to create the space for me to focus on sharing my gifts and to work primarily in my zone of genius has been significant.

The key to cultivating meaningful relationships is ensuring you're in the right rooms. Do you enjoy being there? Does it light you up to be there? You're spending time there, so can you add value by being there? Do you enjoy the conversations? Does it make your brain start to think about other opportunities and possibilities? Is it something that you look forward to?

With the people that I've been fortunate to have great relationships with, I absolutely look forward to all the conversations and all the engagement. It has dramatically changed the types of questions I ask, it has unleashed unforeseen potential and has expanded and amplified my vision for what's in store.

———————————

Looking ahead, what are your aspirations for the future impact of your business, and how do you plan to continue evolving and innovating in this area?

I have big goals for what lies ahead!

So I've spent the vast majority of my life in the Bay Area, right in the heart of Silicon Valley. While the initial part of my chiropractic and nutrition practice was exclusively in my clinic, I then also started working with local corporations regarding ergonomics. Just as I was super excited to see the interrelationship between structure and function in the body, I felt like I had been given backstage VIP access once I started going onsite to talk with various employees at these companies.

I got to witness first-hand how repetitive daily behaviors were actually being executed, with seemingly small stressors like the keyboard perhaps being an inch too high, or someone with a half-eaten lunch on their desk because they were too busy to eat, or observing how people fidget when they're not comfortable.

The experience gave me incredible insight into how and why people would present in my practice with the "sudden onset" of waking up with a stiff neck or pain with bending down to tie one's shoes.

> *We often forget the details of what we're doing because it has become normal and because we're focused on the tasks at hand.*

I think it's human nature to use pain or the presence of any symptom as an indication of our health, but the reality is that our health dashboard has a number of metrics to consider. For so long, we have been living in a world of managing sick-care as our main health-care system. So, **I'm on a mission to change the perception of COMMON symptoms being NORMAL.**

Whether I'm working with:

> a couple having challenges conceiving
> a pregnant mama dealing with nausea, fatigue, or back pain during pregnancy

a postpartum mom dealing with insomnia and
depression
a newborn with latching difficulties
a child who has eczema and allergies
a teen dealing with PMS symptoms
a mom needing multiple cups of coffee just to
have enough energy to get through her day
a dad taking meds to manage chronic headaches
and developing carpal tunnel syndrome
a grandparent suffering from arthritis,

...we have accepted these COMMON symptoms to be
NORMAL. However, it is important to recognize that
"common" *does not*, in fact, equal normal. If it was
normal, then EVERYONE would experience it.

My vision is to continue working with even more
families and communities, helping to regulate the
nervous system within my chiropractic practice, and
virtually through functional nutrition coaching. I
envision working with many more corporations, to be
able to help create stronger wellness programs for
employees and presenting on more stages to shift
how we think about our health and recognize our
potential.

Have you ever sprained your ankle, making you limp
around and change how you walk, shifting more

weight to the other leg? Then the non-injured leg starts to hurt because it's overworked?

Sometimes, we have to remember the childhood song, "Your foot bone is connected to your leg bone, your leg bone is connected to your hip bone..." Our body has so many amazing interwoven relationships that it is virtually impossible to address only one singular aspect and expect that it won't affect somewhere else.

I love helping people connect the dots between the ways in which we move/don't move, the things we eat/don't eat, and the day-to-day management of our thoughts and mental stress.

To me, this is what starts to have the greatest impact on the rest of our body and, ultimately, how we show up each day and impact not only our own lives but also all those around us in countless ways.

"THE PRIVILEGE OF A LIFETIME IS TO
BECOME WHO YOU TRULY ARE."

Carl Jung

embracing change

EMPOWERING TEAMS THROUGH EMOTIONAL INTELLIGENCE AND ARTIFICIAL INTELLIGENCE

AMMIE MICHAELS

in /ammiemichaels

wolfpackhr.com

Ammie Michaels, the visionary behind WolfpackHR, has established a unique niche in the HR consulting industry by specializing in AI integration for small businesses and scaling entrepreneurs. As an HR consultant, she quickly identified a critical gap: traditional consulting firms often overlook the specific needs of these businesses for learning and development, leaving them without leadership and training opportunities.

Ammie founded WolfpackHR with a mission to bridge the gap between traditional HR practices and the transformative potential of AI. As a certified AI specialist and business consultant, she is at the forefront of integrating AI into the workplace. Ammie expertly guides entrepreneurs and businesses in combining human intelligence and AI, giving them a significant competitive edge.

Since launching WolfpackHR, Ammie has been dedicated to supporting both businesses and their team members. She provides comprehensive training and professional development to teams, ensuring they are equipped to thrive in an AI-enhanced environment. Ammie's approach emphasizes the critical importance of communication, connection, and collaboration. She understands that these elements, along with emotional intelligence and emotional regulation, are what distinguish human intelligence from artificial intelligence and are essential for building high-performing teams.

Ammie is deeply committed to helping businesses and entrepreneurs leverage AI ethically and effectively. She believes it's her duty to provide them with the knowledge and tools they need to navigate and excel in a rapidly changing landscape. Her hands-on, empathetic approach makes complex AI concepts accessible and empowers teams to integrate these technologies seamlessly into their daily operations.

Outside WolfpackHR, Ammie enjoys traveling and creating lasting memories with her family and her two Weimaraners, Willow and Winnie. This balance of work and play fuels her creativity and enriches her approach to business. To connect with Ammie and learn more about her journey and expertise in AI, use the contact information above.

How do you define impact?

Impact is my word of the year, and it means everything to me. Typically, if you look up the word 'impact' in the dictionary, you'll find mostly negative connotations. But to me, impact means leaving something forever changed from what it once was, in a positive way.

Impact starts with transforming how we interact with the world and each other. As an entrepreneur, I believe I can impact the world with my life and change the course of future generations. I aim to be a model of an impactful business owner and leader for my kids. My goal is to impact their mindsets and futures by breaking generational cycles of dysfunction, limiting beliefs, control, and judgment that carried on in my previous generations. I want to replace that with examples of unconditional love, kindness, healing, unlimited possibilities, openness, and acceptance.

This definition of impact extends to my professional life too. At WolfpackHR, we're committed to making a positive impact on businesses and individuals. I started WolfpackHR because I saw a critical gap in the traditional consulting structure—one that wasn't accessible or sustainable for small businesses, startups, and scaling entrepreneurs due to the high hundreds-of-dollars-per-hour billable rates. These traditional firms often didn't offer customized services or learning, development, and leadership programs tailored to this audience. As an entrepreneur myself with a background in HR and learning and development, I knew I could fill this gap.

WolfpackHR is built on the values I hold dear: integrity, honesty, kindness, and freedom. We embody the characteristics of a wolf pack— curiosity, bravery, resourcefulness, persistence, empathy, playfulness, patience, strategic thinking, independence, and resilience. These values drive our approach and help us create a world of connection, love, and commitment. I consider myself a joyful, connected, and passionate leader, dedicated to fostering environments where these qualities thrive.

We offer flat-rate services and pricing, making high-quality consulting accessible and predictable for smaller businesses. This approach allows us to provide the necessary support without the financial burden of traditional consulting fees. We've also adapted to changes in the market, especially with advancements in AI. We're proud to be the first firm in the US to certify our entire team in AI, putting us at the forefront of integrating artificial intelligence into business practices. This is crucial as we navigate the seismic shifts in how businesses operate post-pandemic.

At WolfpackHR, we emphasize the importance of communication, connection, and collaboration. We understand that these elements, along with emotional intelligence and emotional regulation, distinguish human intelligence from artificial intelligence and are essential for building high-performing teams. I believe businesses are only as effective as their teams' capabilities and the tools they use. That's why we help small businesses, startups, and scaling entrepreneurs master their teams' emotional intelligence while strategically implementing AI tools. This combination gives them the ultimate competitive advantage in their industry.

Looking back over your life, who has impacted you most, and what specific advice or guidance from them has not only influenced your personal growth but also significantly impacted the direction of your professional career?

Reflecting on this question, I can say without hesitation that my husband, Jon, has impacted me the most throughout my life. His unwavering support, guidance, and partnership have been instrumental in both my personal growth and professional development.

Jon and I met when we were young, and we've grown together through life's challenges and triumphs. His belief in me, even when I doubted myself, has been a constant source of strength. He encouraged me to pursue higher education, supporting me as we both worked our way through undergraduate and graduate degrees as non-traditional students while raising our family.

One of the most impactful pieces of advice Jon has given me is to never stop learning and growing. He's always pushed me to step out of my comfort zone and take risks, which played a significant role in my decision to start WolfpackHR. His unwavering support has been what has kept me going as I've navigated the challenges of building and growing my business.

While Jon has been the primary positive influence in my life, I also recognize the impact my parents had on me, albeit in a different way. Their limited mindsets, education, and emotional intelligence showed me how I could be more prepared to be a parent myself and how to provide a better life for my kids. Observing their struggles motivated me to break the cycle, pursue higher education, and create a more emotionally intelligent and financially stable environment for my own family.

This contrast between the limiting beliefs I grew up with and the growth mindset Jon has helped me cultivate has significantly shaped my personal and professional journey. It's influenced my passion for helping others overcome their own limiting beliefs and create positive transformations in their lives and careers.

The impact Jon has had on my life extends far beyond our personal relationship. His support and guidance have directly influenced the creation and direction of WolfpackHR, shaping our focus on continuous learning and personal growth, while having fun at the same time. His impact is woven into the fabric of our company culture and the services we provide to our clients.

———

Think about the personal challenges you've overcome in your life. How did the obstacles that you've overcome play a part in the impact that you make now?

Growing up in a financially strained environment where independence was a necessity, I learned the value of perseverance and self-reliance early on. Our household was often marked by scarcity and uncertainty. We shopped at second-hand stores and dealt with frequent car troubles. I remember the frustration of pushing our old car to the side of the road and the embarrassment of shopping for back-to-school clothes in thrift stores that smelled of must and age. These experiences instilled in me a determination to provide a different life for my own family. My husband and I were nontraditional students who juggled work, school, and family life for many, many years. We wanted to provide our kids with opportunities we didn't have. Our efforts resulted in a lifestyle vastly different from our own upbringings.

Despite our hard work and education, I still faced professional setbacks like layoffs as an educated professional. This uncertainty highlighted the importance of taking control of my own career and diversifying my earning potential. I dove into learning about personal finance, investing, and credit management, empowering myself with knowledge that isn't really taught or talked about.

Starting WolfpackHR was my way of taking charge and creating something meaningful. I saw a gap in how traditional consulting firms served small businesses, startups, and scaling entrepreneurs. Their rigid structures and high fees were often inaccessible. With WolfpackHR, I wanted to provide affordable, flat-rate, and sustainable consulting that these businesses could rely on. More importantly, I aimed to make professional development playful and fun, using innovative approaches. My goal is to empower these businesses, helping them thrive without the heavy burden of conventional consulting costs, and to transform their learning experiences into something joyful and transformative.

The obstacles I've faced have taught me the value of education, the necessity of financial independence, and the importance of creating accessible, impactful solutions for those often overlooked by traditional services.

Reflect on a moment in your professional life that you perceived as a failure. How did this experience lead to your most significant lessons of impact? Share how you have applied these lessons to positively influence your life and the lives of others.

Early in my career, I faced a challenging moment that would shape my approach to leadership and personal growth. A boss pulled me aside one day and told me I needed to change my attitude. Initially, I was shocked and immediately felt undervalued and underappreciated. I always thought I was a good employee, but he wasn't referring to my work product, he was referring to the fact that I was wearing my heart on my sleeve, and it was creating a toxic environment.

I REALIZED I COULDN'T LEAD OTHERS IF I COULDN'T LEAD MYSELF.

I realized I couldn't lead others if I couldn't lead myself. I needed to manage my emotions and do some deep self-reflection and soul-searching. I also learned that I was operating on autopilot with the mindset and beliefs from my childhood. Emotional regulation was not modeled for me in my household growing up. Even though I went through higher education, it didn't change those hard-set patterns subconsciously set in my mind from when I was younger.

This feedback was a wake-up call, prompting me to embark on a journey of deep self-reflection and emotional growth. I had to learn to manage my emotions and lead by example. This transformation allowed me to develop a leadership style centered on empathy, emotional regulation, and authentic connection—principles that now define my approach to business and team development.

Today, I apply these lessons in my work with clients at WolfpackHR. I emphasize the importance of emotional intelligence in leadership and provide tools and strategies for managing emotions effectively. By helping others develop these skills, I aim to foster workplaces that are not only more productive but also more compassionate and supportive. This focus on emotional intelligence and authentic leadership is a cornerstone of the transformative work we do at WolfpackHR.

What role do partnerships and collaborations play in amplifying the impact of your business? How do you identify and cultivate meaningful relationships with other business leaders?

As I've become an entrepreneur, I quickly recognized that I can't do everything alone. Collaboration is a cornerstone of my approach to business. I quickly realized early in establishing the business that I couldn't do everything alone. Building a network of partners and collaborators has been crucial to the success of WolfpackHR. These relationships amplify our impact and allow us to serve our clients more effectively.

I seek partnerships with individuals and organizations that align with my mission-driven and heart-centered values. Aligning with others who are committed to making a positive impact is essential to me. This philosophy is also reflected in my involvement with the Women's Impact Network (WIN), where I support fellow female entrepreneurs and business owners in achieving their goals.

In cultivating these relationships, I look for partners who share a passion for making a difference and who have demonstrated a commitment to ethical practices. I believe that true collaboration is built on mutual respect, shared values, and a common vision. By working together, we can achieve more than we ever could on our own.

Partnerships also provide opportunities for learning and growth. I am constantly inspired by the innovative ideas and diverse perspectives of my collaborators. These interactions challenge me to think differently and push the boundaries of what's possible. Through collaboration, we can create synergies that enhance our collective impact and drive meaningful change in our communities and beyond.

Looking ahead, what are your aspirations for the future impact of your business, and how do you plan to continue evolving and innovating in this area?

Looking to the future, my aspirations for WolfpackHR are both ambitious and deeply rooted in our mission to create positive change. My dream is to continue helping others by bringing play into professional development, creating happier and healthier work environments. I want to assist individuals and organizations in making positive transformations that impact not only their professional lives but their personal relationships as well.

One of the key areas we focus on for innovation is integrating AI technology with human-centered approaches. As the first firm in the US to certify our entire team in AI, we're leading the way in this integration. We plan to keep evolving our services to help businesses leverage AI effectively while maintaining a strong focus on human skills like emotional intelligence, creativity, and adaptability.

Environmental sustainability is another passion of mine. I am deeply committed to making a measurable impact on the environment and helping to slow or reverse climate change. At WolfpackHR, we plan to support environmental initiatives that protect and preserve our planet. This includes investing in reforestation efforts, renewable energy sources, sustainable agriculture, and reducing food waste. Clean air and water are essential for all living beings, and we're exploring partnerships with organizations like The Nature Conservancy to amplify our impact in these areas.

I also aim to build a lasting legacy for my children, instilling values of empowerment, sustainability, and the importance of human connection. I want to change their generational money story and provide them with a planet they can be proud of.

This legacy is about more than financial stability—it's about creating a world where they can thrive and contribute positively.

In terms of business growth, I envision WolfpackHR becoming a leader in ethical and sustainable business practices, setting an example for other companies to follow. We're developing new workshops and training programs that combine professional development with social impact. For instance, we're working on a workshop that not only teaches new skills but also contributes to expanding renewable energy efforts, potentially providing renewable power sources for homeless and underprivileged communities.

Innovation will remain at the heart of our evolution. We'll continue to stay at the forefront of HR trends and technologies, always looking for new ways to make workplaces more human-centered, efficient, and fulfilling. This might involve developing new AI-powered tools for strategic business operations or creating more immersive and engaging training experiences.

Ultimately, my aspiration is for WolfpackHR to be a catalyst for widespread positive change in the business world. I want us to play a significant role in shaping a future where businesses prioritize people and the planet alongside profit, where work is a source of fulfillment and growth, and where the power of human potential is fully realized and celebrated.

By continuing to innovate, collaborate, and stay true to our core values, I believe we can create a ripple effect of positive impact that extends far beyond our immediate clients and into the broader fabric of society. This is the legacy I hope to build—**a legacy of transformation, sustainability, and human-centered progress.**

For more insights and to connect with me, visit ammiemichaels.com or wolfpackhr.com.

the impact of community in action

LAUREN LUEDEKE

in /lauren-luedeke

bylaurenjean.com

Lauren Luedeke specializes in working with small to medium e-commerce businesses that are ready to scale but lack the resources to hire a full-time, in-house email specialist. As an experienced email consultant, Lauren advises on best practices for deliverability, campaign frequency, and, most importantly, converting subscribers into paying customers.

Unlike many consultants who move from gig to gig, Lauren prides herself on building long-term relationships with her clients. These enduring partnerships have allowed her to support clients through all stages of their business and email programs.

Lauren and her team have successfully launched email programs from scratch, starting with zero contacts, and managed mature programs with over 250,000 contacts, generating hundreds of thousands of dollars annually through email alone.

When she is not building or analyzing email funnels, Lauren enjoys spending time with her husband, two kids, and their hyper puppy.

How do you define impact?

When I think of impact, a few words come to mind: change, influence, drive, and personal responsibility. It represents an overall attitude toward life and how one's actions leave a lasting impression, whether positive or negative.

Impact embodies impressions left through actions. Actions always speak louder than words, and they give us the opportunity to make a difference.

Looking back over your life, who has impacted you most, and what specific advice or guidance from them has not only influenced your personal growth but also significantly impacted the direction of your professional career?

When I look in the rearview mirror, each friend, family member, mentor, and manager has taught me something that led me to where I am today.

When I think about where I am as a business owner today, two individuals stand out who significantly impacted the direction of my professional career. Not only did they give me tons of advice, but what stood out was their willingness to take a chance on me.

My father introduced me to Brad, a successful businessperson and owner of a small e-commerce company selling safety products. After meeting for the first time over coffee, Brad hired me on the spot with absolutely zero e-commerce experience. Despite the products not being glamorous, I was eager to dive into the e-commerce world, ready to learn and grow.

I was just 23 when Brad entrusted me with managing responsibilities I was definitely not yet qualified for—from P&L management and customer service to overseeing suppliers and marketing. This was not a typical entry-level job; his trust in me was both daunting and empowering. He allowed me the space to make plenty of mistakes and learn, a responsibility that initially made me uneasy.

As it turned out, the impact of those mistakes and the opportunities they presented led me to where I am today.

The second person who played a pivotal role in my career is Karen, a powerhouse who started working for another business Brad owned a year and a half after I started.

Brad always praised Karen's ability to execute strategy. **It didn't take me long to realize I needed**

to learn everything I could from her. And Brad was right. Karen's leadership, strategic thinking, and ability to express her opinions profoundly shaped my aspirations and career goals.

A year later, Karen left to start her own business. At the time, I didn't realize her move would be pivotal in MY career. Soon after she left, she convinced me to start my own business.

Because of her, I took the leap and became an e-commerce email consultant at the ripe old age of 26. It was a decision that came out of the blue, something I had NEVER considered, and yet, it felt like the most natural step to take.

And it didn't stop there. Karen has helped me land a handful of my clients by recommending me and assisting me with the ins and outs of successfully serving them, and so much more. We share clients and strategize together to this day.

As for Brad, he has been a client on and off over the years, and he's always just a phone call away.

Brad and Karen saw something in me I hadn't recognized in myself—the potential to excel in e-commerce and entrepreneurship. Their belief in me and willingness to mentor and support me have been transformative. They didn't just influence my career; they ignited a passion and instilled the confidence to pursue my path and help small businesses needing my skills.

Their impact resonates in every decision I make and every client I serve. I am deeply grateful for their guidance, belief in me, and enduring friendship. One day, I hope to do the same for someone else to encourage a ripple effect of positive impact.

Think about the personal challenges you've overcome in your life. How did the obstacles that you've overcome play a part in the impact that you make now?

I never saw it coming.

I was a college athlete who kept herself active with half-marathons and sprint triathlons. And all of a sudden, simple tasks like walking or opening jars became excruciatingly painful. I started losing large chunks of hair and watched them go down the shower drain. I struggled with chronic fatigue, often sleeping excessively just to make it through the workweek. I was diagnosed with a lifelong, chronic disease at 25 years old.

Lupus completely reshaped my life and transformed who I am today.

Two days stand out to me as turning points. One morning, when I woke up to get ready for work, I couldn't get my legs to move. As much as I tried, I couldn't stand up. Thankfully, I was living with my parents, and I remember lying there knowing that my dad would go downstairs at a particular time to start his morning for work. I waited 45 minutes and yelled for him through my door when I heard him in the hall. When I told my dad, he started crying. We both realized the harsh reality of what I was dealing with.

The second turning point was the time I did my weekly routine of filling my pill pack. Just as I filled up my Tuesday night pills, I realized how many I had to take—16 of them. Tears just started flowing.

I couldn't help but wonder about the future. Would my health continue to decline? If this was what 25 looked like, what would 55 or 65 look like? How would this affect my loved ones, especially the man I had met less than a year before? Would I be able to get off the medication that prevented me from having children?

Determined to regain control over my life, I embarked on a journey to heal. Despite skepticism from others, I made drastic changes to my diet and lifestyle.

By the end of 2015, these changes began to yield tangible improvements in my health, reducing the frequency of debilitating flare-ups and restoring a sense of normalcy.

The journey wasn't without its challenges. But on the hard days, I remembered that my life and the dream of having children depended on me improving.

Through perseverance and unwavering support from my family and husband—the man I mentioned above—we welcomed our daughter in May 2020 and our son in May 2022. They are daily reminders of the adversity I have overcome and my gratitude for not letting lupus dictate my fate.

My doctor says I'll live with lupus forever. But I am determined to find a way to reverse it completely. And with how far I have come, taking only one pill a day to control my lupus, and I know it's not impossible.

The impact of my illness and the need to focus on my health and find balance play a huge role in my business. In fact, I have built one of my company values around it:

> **Well-Being First:** We prioritize our health and families, understanding that a strong personal foundation enables us to perform at our best. By ensuring our well-being, we can better serve each other, our clients, and the world around us effectively and with genuine care.

I'll be the first to admit that I sometimes forget this value when things get hectic. However, setting it as a core value for the business holds me and my team accountable for our actions. It's that important.

————

Reflect on a moment in your professional life that you perceived as a failure. How did this experience lead to your most significant lessons of impact? Share how you have applied these lessons to positively influence your life and the lives of others.

Early in my entrepreneurial journey, a client hired my team to build a company website in close collaboration with their marketing director.

About three-quarters into the project, the director unexpectedly disappeared, leaving me to meet the owners for the first time.

Our progress updates with the marketing director had been positive, so I was completely unprepared when we sat down with the business owners. Within minutes, they tore into our work, criticized me personally, and demanded a refund right then and there. It was a gut punch that shook my confidence as a business owner and affected my bottom line. (I lost a lot of money on that project!)

Initially, this failure was a sensitive topic for me. Still, after some time, I consciously decided to remove the emotion from it and see it as a teaching moment, recognizing setbacks as opportunities for growth and refinement.

This challenging situation taught me how important thicker skin is in business and that your work is not for everybody.

Building trust and mutual understanding are non-negotiable for me. That's why I've fine-tuned our team's business practices to set clear expectations and prevent misunderstandings. For instance, we have a more detailed contract outlining the project scope and deliverables—something I should have done in the first place!

I've also learned to proactively manage client expectations, ensuring we are on the same page throughout the project. These changes have helped us avoid similar situations and strengthened our client relationships.

How do you ensure your business practices align with ethical and sustainable principles while balancing profitability with making a positive impact?

My commitment to ethical business practices was first challenged when I had to present my summa cum laude thesis. It involved delivering a convincing case to three professors who had to unanimously agree on its merit, regardless of their personal beliefs.

My thesis focused on the unethical marketing of cigarettes and tobacco. This issue was deeply personal to me as my grandmother passed away from lung cancer caused by smoking before I was born. During my presentation, I stated I would never support a client whose business practices I didn't ethically believe in, like cigarettes and tobacco products.

After I presented my thesis, I awkwardly discovered that one of the professors had previously worked in the marketing department of a cigarette company. I practically told my professor to his face that I believed he did something unethical. Yikes. Despite this, the panel unanimously agreed my arguments were convincing and sound, allowing me to graduate summa cum laude.

The impact of this exercise has stuck with me; I constantly think about it when I meet with potential clients. I am proud to say I have kept my commitment and turned down several opportunities because of my convictions. If I don't ethically believe in their marketing or selling practices, I will not take them on as clients, regardless of the paycheck size.

For instance, I once declined a job that focused on a controversial topic because I wasn't sure of my stance. As my beliefs evolved, I realized I made the right choice since I didn't align with the values the job required. This experience underscored the importance of aligning my work with my ethics, a lesson I carry in every decision.

A skilled marketer can market anything, but someone who genuinely believes in a company's product or service can make all the difference. My commitment to a client's cause increases the potential for profitability and makes a positive impact.

I can fully support their goals and create meaningful marketing strategies by prioritizing clients and projects that align with my values. This alignment leads to more authentic and compelling marketing efforts, which drive better results for my clients and my business, reinforcing the value of ethical business practices. Once again, it is a ripple effect of positive impact.

What role do partnerships and collaborations play in amplifying the impact of your business? How do you identify and cultivate meaningful relationships with other business leaders?

As a contractor who hires other contractors, partnerships, and collaborations are the backbone of my business. I intentionally built it this way to ensure everyone operates within their zone of genius.

Digital marketing is an ever-evolving field, with new industry standards and best practices emerging rapidly. It would be impossible for one person to keep up with all these changes across various digital channels. Think of how often Google updates its algorithms. Empowering someone who focuses solely on SEO ensures we stay on top of these changes and maintain our clients' competitive edge.

By hiring specialists, I ensure that each digital channel is managed by someone who is up to speed with the latest trends and has the creative bandwidth to innovate. Our work is not just a transaction but a true collaboration with a sense of camaraderie. We work as a team to connect all the dots across each channel. Without these partnerships, I wouldn't have the business I have now.

Many of my successful partnerships today result from how I foster networking and cultivate meaningful relationships. My approach to networking does not involve attending a handful of events and exchanging business cards, hoping someone will remember me later. Instead, I build genuine relationships with people who see beyond transactions. Often, it's about connecting with those who understand the challenges of running a small business and align with my values.

And that's where the Elevate 360 mastermind has come in, allowing me to expand my close-knit network. I'll be the first to admit that the main thing I was looking for from the mastermind was how it could help me maximize the bottom line with what I already built and take me to the "next level," and networking was secondary.

Instead, networking with other masterminds has given me the confidence to innovate and try new things to streamline the business, allowing me to spend more time with my family. The new approaches indirectly strengthened my business and gave me the support I didn't realize I needed. Deep down, I have a feeling there will be a partnership down the road with one of the members, but the sense of community it gave me has made all the difference.

———

Looking ahead, what are your aspirations for the future impact of your business, and how do you plan to continue evolving and innovating in this area?

As I envision the future of my business, my thoughts turn to my family.

THIS IS MY WHY.

The other day, I was lying with my 4-year-old daughter, discussing her school routine. Our mornings have always been challenging, with her tearful goodbyes as I leave for work. While I know she enjoys school and is thriving, her cries for Mama often leave me questioning my role as a business owner. (I'm sure many parents can relate to this struggle.)

Recently, she expressed what upset her about attending school even though she enjoyed it: "Because I know I won't see you for a long time once I say goodbye." And she is right. Most days, she is at school from 8 a.m. to 5 p.m. That's a long time for a 4-year-old and my 2-year-old son!

This is my WHY.

Contrary to the popular belief that you're either an at-work parent or a stay-at-home parent, I aspire to be both. (Note: Parenting itself is a full-time job!) I am committed to building a business that allows me to find harmony and be present for my family while driving its success.

I dream of picking up my kids once the school day is done and avoiding aftercare so we don't have to spend so much time apart. I aspire to be present with them instead of being preoccupied with a to-do list to serve my clients. I want to see their smiles at ballet or T-ball instead of staring at the ceiling feeling overstimulated and run down like I have been since they were born. It won't always be butterflies and rainbows, but I am committed to making these moments the norm.

Without the many privileges I have been given, these desires wouldn't feel within reach. Because of that, I want my business to open the doors of privilege for others, enabling them to reach their desires.

Through my business, I aim to empower my team to have the freedom and flexibility to build lives beyond the office and extend this impact to my clients. By prioritizing well-being, I work to produce a tangible, positive difference in the lives of my clients, teammates, and family.

With these efforts, I firmly believe we can create a positive ripple effect, empowering each person we touch to make a significant difference in the lives of others.

*from immigrant to
impact maker*

GISELLE CARSON, ESQ.

in /gisellecarsonimmigration

marksgray.com/attorneys/giselle-carson

Giselle Carson, Esq. is a dynamic U.S. corporate immigration and compliance attorney, known for her proactive, responsive, and engaging approach to partnering with the C-Suite, HR, and Legal leaders to navigate U.S. immigration and secure work visas and green cards for global talent.

Author of *Beyond the H-1B: A Guide to Work Visa Options*, and founder of her corporate immigration practice, her passion extends beyond legal realms. She has successfully crossed many finish lines in her professional and personal journey with resilience and determination.

In addition to over two decades of legal expertise dedicated to corporate immigration law, she is a two-time immigrant, a global marathoner, an Ironman triathlete, and a River City DWTS ambassador. She is a graduate of Leadership Florida and Leadership Jacksonville.

Giselle goes beyond legal representation, infusing her work with personal experiences, boundless energy, and unwavering passion.

How do you define impact?

Our government has made the immigration process political, complicated, and harsh. The process is an emotional drain.

For me, impact is our ability to transform that process. I'm using my legal knowledge positive energy, and empathy to transform our workplaces, workforce, and world.

As a corporate immigration attorney, I'm privileged to empower the C-suite, HR, and legal leaders with the knowledge and tools to successfully navigate the complexities and craziness of our immigration laws.

I'm grateful to be able to leverage my legal experience and life journeys as an immigrant from Cuba to Canada to the United States and endurance athlete to positively impact my community, clients and country.

My team and I partner with enterprising employers to prepare and file work visas and green cards for highly skilled foreign workers. Persistent labor shortages and declining birth rates are leaving the U.S. in dire need of skilled workers. Our work ensures a robust and sustainable workforce that advances the strength of our economy and the competitiveness of our country.

Looking back over your life, who has impacted you most, and what specific advice or guidance from them has not only influenced your personal growth but also significantly impacted the direction of your professional career?

I'm very grateful for the many generous people who have mentored, supported, and cheered me during the course of my life and who have contributed to who I am today.

Two remarkable ladies stand out for their profound influence on my personal growth and professional direction: my grandmothers, Mella and Ana.

Mella, my maternal grandmother, was the epitome of determination, passion, and resourcefulness. In her 60s, she left her familiar life in Cuba and came to the U.S. with my aunt, uncle, and cousin to help them immigrate and assimilate to the United States. Then, in her 70s, she did the same for us in Canada.

She spoke no English or French but managed our household in Montreal so my parents could work, and I could go to school. For her, it was paramount that my mom, my aunt, and I could obtain a professional degree—which she never could.

Her ability to navigate new environments with determination, charm and savvy, making friends wherever she went, shaped my approach to life and work. When people comment on my level of determination, I'm honored to say, "Yes, from my grandmother's genes"

Ana, my paternal grandmother, lived in Cardenas, Cuba. I saw her less because it was difficult to travel to see her. I would often spend the summers with her. My grandfather and her were up very early to attend to many things and visitors. She exemplified strength and compassion. Managing a busy household on a farm, she coordinated meals and space for many with grace and calm.

At times, there were 10 or more of us kids and many visitors. The beds and food were limited, but She managed it all with grace. Of course, she had challenges, but we didn't see them. Her resilience and warm spirit were deeply inspiring. She died after I left Cuba. I was never able to say goodbye. I never saw her again.

Today, I carry their legacies in my heart and actions. Mella's determination and resourcefulness are reflected in how I've built my immigration practice from the ground up. Ana's strength and empathy guide me as I manage my team and client relations. Their influences are the foundation of my professional and personal life and drive me to lead with strength and heart.

———————

Think about the personal challenges you've overcome in your life. How did the obstacles that you've overcome play a part in the impact that you make now?

IT FEELS SURREAL, LIKE A DREAM YOU CAN'T WAKE UP FROM. BUT THIS WAS MY REALITY.

Picture this: you're 15 years old, and in the blink of an eye, everything familiar vanishes. Your friends, your language, your culture, your very home—all replaced by an unsettling silence of the unknown.

It feels surreal, like a dream you can't wake up from. But this was my reality.

At 15 years old, I discovered that my parents had made a life-altering decision: to flee Cuba and seek asylum in Canada.

We arrived with nothing but our resilience and hopes for a new beginning. Montreal welcomed us, but it demanded a complete reinvention of everything I knew.

I forged new friendships, learned new languages, and embraced unfamiliar landscapes amidst snowflakes, a stark contrast to the sunny streets of Cuba.

After several years in Canada, I was thrilled to obtain a bachelor's degree in Physical Therapy, Marry an ingenious and witty gent, and have a new outlook on life.

With renewed energy, we moved to Florida. This move wasn't just geographical; it was, again, the start of a new chapter. With not much more than a professional degree, a U-Haul trailer of possessions, and a bright outlook, my journey in the United States began from scratch, again.

Law school came next. I set aside a rewarding career in physical therapy and embraced the complexities of law. I started as a litigator in medical malpractice defense at my current firm, but it wasn't long before I discovered my true passion: Immigration law, boosted by awesome coffee.

Corporate immigration was an area no one at the firm handled, so I took it upon myself to learn. Nights spent poring over books translated into days attending courses, each moment a step closer to my calling of being the founder of our corporate immigration practice and growing it to service enterprising employers, initially just me and currently a team of six.

Among these professional transformations, I found an unexpected outlet: endurance events. After a casual suggestion, I went from never running a marathon to completing 25 across five continents—including Antarctica—and completing five triathlons, including The Kona Confidence. Each event, each race, is a testament to the endurance, curiosity, and confidence I have cultivated into epic athletics and dancing since those early unsettling days.

These experiences—my migrations, academic and professional shifts, and ventures into extreme athletics—have not just shaped who I am; they propel me forward. With each step, I open new doors, ready to embrace whatever challenges and opportunities lie ahead.

Reflect on a moment in your professional life that you perceived as a failure. How did this experience lead to your most significant lessons of impact? Share how you have applied these lessons to positively influence your life and the lives of others.

A nerve-wracking experience in my professional life was the losing and rebuilding of my team after years of stability building the practice.

The resignation of one team member triggered a domino effect, leaving me with a dwindling team and wonderful clients to serve who relied on us. This unexpected disruption felt like a huge failure, plunging me into months of painful rumination.

The necessity to rehire, train, and empower the new team was filled with clumsiness and self-questioning. I questioned my goals, my purpose, and my impact. The process led me to soul-searching and ultimately reaffirmed my commitment to the person I was becoming, to the future of my practice, and to its impact.

Drawing parallels to my marathon experiences— where my first grueling race left me limping for several days, yet by the third, I had found my stride—I re-embraced the discomfort of growth.

While painful, these events were catalysts for new beginnings. They led me to innovate, expand my perspective, approach challenges with renewed vigor, and remember that **comfort doesn't lead to growth.**

The ordeal tested my resilience and brought me to rekindle practices like mindfulness, meditation, and yoga—vital tools that supported me through these trials. It also highlighted the invaluable role of mentors, my family, and community support during such transformative times.

In hindsight, this period of loss and setbacks was a preparation for a new level of expansion, empathy, and learning. It has infused me with a new level of self-confidence, discipline, and lightness.

I'm grateful for my team, clients, family and community. I remind myself and them to consistently focus on the brightness of our sunshine and positive future. The shadows will always be there, ready to cast worries over us.

This experience is also a reminder that failures are learning opportunities and an important part of our journeys.

Growth requires us to release, create space, and embrace the unknown.

It's within our power to choose how we respond—for me, I needed to reclaim my optimistic energy.

Today, I'm not aiming to survive, but to evolve and thrive. I'm embracing, with passion and unique style, a future with my team filled with exciting potential lit by the impact that we are making.

———————

How do you ensure your business practices align with ethical and sustainable principles while balancing profitability with making a positive impact?

Maintaining ethical integrity and sustainability in business, especially in the complex field of corporate immigration, requires a vigilant balance between profitability and positive impact.

When I first launched my practice, I accepted a more diverse array of cases. This was partly out of necessity—to gain experience and establish the practice—but it was also due to not yet having honed in on my true passion.

As I developed the practice and our brand, I moved exclusively to corporate immigration because I believe in the critical role of foreign talent and a diverse workforce in bringing innovation and resilience to businesses and our economy.

The landscape of immigration law changes daily, and recognizing this is crucial to maintaining my ethical standards.

To stay within the ethical realm of things, you just have to know what is right and what is wrong, then defend your position.

A key aspect of my approach is determining which cases to accept. Unlike others in the field who might take any case that comes in, I choose to refer out cases where I lack knowledge or experience. Since the beginning of the year, I have referred out over 30 cases. This selective process ensures that my team and I are the best for the cases we take on.

What role do partnerships and collaborations play in amplifying the impact of your business? How do you identify and cultivate meaningful relationships with other business leaders?

Partnerships and collaborations are essential to amplifying the impact of our work and life. They allow us to reach and grow beyond our immediate circles and capabilities. A fun and very impactful example of this is my involvement for five years and ongoing as an Ambassador of the Jacksonville Children's Chorus, particularly through their local 'Dancing with the Stars' inspired fundraiser.

For this annual event, community leaders are partnered with a professional dancer—then, we choose our music, choreography and outfits and commit to rigorous choreography and dance practice.

This initiative is the essence of impactful partnerships and collaborations. As we collaborate to put together an amazing dance performance, we also develop meaningful relationships with other business leaders and engage in significant fundraising efforts for the benefit of the chorus and children.

The discipline, teamwork, and shared mission of supporting local children's arts education are profound. My team and I embody these values in our practice when working with our clients and other business leaders: identifying shared goals, committing to mutual success, and learning from each interaction.

This approach has taught me that the most meaningful relationships—whether in dance, law, or any other field—are built on trust, shared vision, and relentless pursuit of excellence.

By aligning with partners who share these values, our corporate immigration practice grows in scope and deepens its impact, helping us empower more businesses and talented foreign workers and make a positive difference in the world.

Looking ahead, what are your aspirations for the future impact of your business, and how do you plan to continue evolving and innovating in this area?

Looking ahead, I see a beautiful future forged from the fires of trial and perseverance—a future where there will be setbacks as preparation for a brighter and more impactful tomorrow. I see a future rich with opportunities for growth, learning, and collaboration.

In my practice, I am providing dynamic, uplifting, and engaging corporate immigration services, complemented by an innovative immigration academy tailored for C-suite, HR, and Legal leaders.

Leveraging my knowledge, energy, and determination, we're creating transformative and innovative learning experiences that emphasize a holistic approach to professional development and well-being.

We embrace the synergy between professional health, wellness, and corporate immigration expertise, which enriches our lives and the lives of others.

We are known for our unique approach to delivering core corporate immigration services alongside tailored workshops, VIP days, podcasts, certifications, and retreats to thousands of leaders. These initiatives help them navigate the complexities of immigration law and enhance their confidence and professional growth.

My active engagement in the community continues to enrich my life, reinforcing the importance of the relationships I've nurtured.

Furthermore, I am on a quest to complete marathons on all seven continents, with only South America and Africa remaining. This challenge fuels my dedication to wellness, balance, and discipline, which energizes and allows me to live my best life.

In the spirit of Maya Angelou's words, my mission extends beyond mere survival. **I aim to thrive with passion, compassion, humor, and style, driving forward the powerful legacy and impact of our work.**

"WE ALL MUST SUFFER FROM ONE OF TWO PAINS: THE PAIN OF DISCIPLINE OR THE PAIN OF REGRET."

Jim Rohn

making the most of your dash

CLAIRE DARR

/claire-hetherington-darr

clairedarr.com

Claire is a former corporate lawyer turned business executive coach who has a passion for guiding business professionals in corporate America to create a life of peace and purpose without giving up their six-seven-figure salary.

Claire believes that understanding your worth comes from within and is the quickest way to create a balanced life and maintain a fulfilling career. Through practical, real-life solutions, Claire passionately teaches how to build massive transformation and impact in life to create a life that you actually want to leap out of bed for every day.

How do you define impact?

Impact is making the most of your dash.

I was born in 1974, and then there's a dash, we don't know what the end date is. It's about what you do in that time with your dash and the impact it makes. We're all given a great opportunity to steward the time, talents, and uniqueness God has given us. For most, impact means going big or going home. For me, it's that, but it's actually about **one life.**

If one person feels the impact of me living in my purpose, then that is the impact I am here to make. It's not one person because the ripple effect goes on and on. So, even if it is just one person, it becomes many.

The ripple effect can be so wonderful that we never even know how many people's lives are changed. We can never quantify it.

Impact doesn't have to be overwhelming. It can be one person, one life.

Looking back over your life, who has impacted you most, and what specific advice or guidance from them has not only influenced your personal growth but also significantly impacted the direction of your professional career?

My grandfather's name was Charles Hare. He died over 25 years ago, and he was such an influence in my life. He lived through both world wars, which are big deals in the UK, and much of his influence was tied to how he showed up in life.

He wasn't educated, as others would say; when he was 12 years old, he was put on a ship to sail the world as a cabin boy. His mother died when he was a baby, so he never knew his mother. He was one of many kids. They didn't have money or food, he experienced extreme poverty.

He lived a life of lack in many ways, yet he went on to survive the Second World War. He was an air-sea rescue man in the Second World War. He taught himself how to speak different languages, play music, and paint, a true Renaissance man.

When I met him as a child in his later life, he'd lived this whole life before I came into the world. All I ever saw from him was peace. He had a calm, steady love of the world. He must have witnessed such hard things in life but didn't show up that way, he didn't let it define him or hold him back.

What he taught me wasn't through words. It was in how he showed up.

He taught me how to show up in a room and be confident. That helped me so much in business, as I became a corporate lawyer, often the only woman in a room surrounded by men. He taught me to show up with quiet confidence, being respectful of people yet knowing that I was there for a reason and my voice mattered.

My grandfather inherently respected people, humanity, and diversity. He was ahead of his time. Through him, I also learned to trust myself. I'm very grateful to have spent 22 years with him on this planet.

His life shows the importance of how we show up. We never know who and how we're impacting people.

———————

Reflect on a moment in your professional life that you perceived as a failure. How did this experience lead to your most significant lessons of impact? Share how you have applied these lessons to positively influence your life and the lives of others.

As I look back on my entire professional life, a lot of learning has happened. I'm in a season of pivoting from working for others in the corporate world to embracing my own business. Acknowledging this wasn't my path is scary. I've been on a journey and learned to listen to my intuition and others.

Now, I've found myself in executive coaching, and I love it. It feels like I'm waking up, living my purpose every day. What got me here was another business. Without it, I wouldn't have had the capacity and confidence to form my own company and start to help others from the coaching perspective.

The hard part with the other business is that I didn't do that well in it. I set many goals and targets over the past few years for that business that I didn't attain.

I had lots of goals and targets that, on paper, I should have reached, and I just didn't. I showed up with the tools I needed, my education, and none of it worked, yet I saw other people "succeeding."

It wasn't for a while that I faced the hard realization that it wasn't for me. I wasn't aligned with the business, and it wasn't bringing me joy; it felt like a struggle.

Walking away at the time meant failure to me. It made me feel like I was giving up and incapable of doing it even though everyone else could. I journaled and meditated on it, and I've finally gotten to peace with that season. It was a really rich and beautiful time that got me to where I am today. I've learned not to look at it like an absolute failure, because it wasn't. It was a branch of my path, a catalyst for my calling.

———————

How do you ensure your business practices align with ethical and sustainable principles while balancing profitability with making a positive impact?

I make sure that what I'm doing is for the collective good so that I can focus on the impact of that *one life*. One person impacted is enough for me.

When I form a great relationship with a client and see their transformation, it's exciting to know that there may be other people down the road who benefit from that. From that one client relationship, the collective good is raised. I start there and remind myself that God is moving me through a lot of this.

DOING THE RIGHT THING FOR THE RIGHT REASONS STANDS THE TEST OF TIME.

I was designed a certain way. I may not ever know every piece of why I am here, but I know that I'm here to collectively help others have an impact, to raise others up.

I already see glimmers of this aligning, and I get to have a very successful life and business while having an impact helping others. Whenever I'm doing something and a little bit of doubt creeps in, I think to myself, *do the next right thing for the next right reason.*

Doing the right thing for the right reasons stands the test of time. That's where sustainability comes in: I can keep showing up and know that I'm aligned and on track with my God-given purpose. This also helps when things don't turn out as I would have hoped, I can hold on to the knowledge that I did it for the right reason. That's so important to me.

I've used this when making difficult decisions such as leaving a job opportunity, turning down an opportunity, saying no to someone, and having tough conversations with people. It's sort of my due North.

For me, staying true to your purpose and mission in life sets you on the right path, even if there isn't evidence available to confirm you're on track. When we're here for the right reason, we can be profitable while also keeping people front and center. That will always feel good and win out in the end.

What role do partnerships and collaborations play in amplifying the impact of your business? How do you identify and cultivate meaningful relationships with other business leaders?

I've not always been a team player. As a child, I didn't like team sports. I was a lone wolf. I liked swimming and solo dancing. I liked things where I was responsible and only had to rely on myself. Whether I won or lost, it was all on me.

My initial career as an attorney rewarded that in many ways. I hate to say it, but a lot of the time, when you're a successful attorney, you are conditioned not to trust others and not to work collaboratively.

It is very much a dog-eat-dog grab for success. What can I do? How can I prove myself? How can I show that I'm a valued person here? It served me well as a non-team player, but deep down, it's not very fun to go it alone and to always have everything resting on your shoulders, win or lose.

Over the past few years, I've done a lot of growth work. I've learned to see and really appreciate the value in other people. In the past, I realized I would go into many conversations wanting to win and always have the last word.

That's certainly great as an attorney. It brought success, but it's not a fun way to live. Over the past few years, I've learned to take a moment and get to know people. Really look and listen to people. To seek to understand others.

Realize that we were all put here with beautiful, unique blueprints. What if we all come together for the greater good? We can only be stronger.

I've learned to go from being a lone wolf to looking at other people, seeing their value, and trusting that we'll have each other's backs. Collectively, we can help others.

I don't have to be the one leading the charge or the best of the best. I can play my part and have someone else play their part, and we all benefit from it. There is so much value in other people. It's foolish not to see that and use that. We are so much stronger together.

It's also important to seek out other people who are aligned. You could all be very different and come with different perspectives, but you're aligned in very similar ways. Lean into that, and continue to show up around people who raise you up. You have to identify and cultivate success in those relationships, but first, you have to seek them out.

———

Looking ahead, what are your aspirations for the future impact of your business, and how do you plan to continue evolving and innovating in this area?

My business is here to help people love and live their lives. So many people aren't, and let's change that. My hope and dream for people is that they get to experience and lean into their desires and dreams and start to dream again. So many of us dreamed as children and then gave that up because it wasn't sensible.

Let's suspend "sensible" and know that we can live full, exciting, beautiful lives now.

We don't need to put off loving our lives until retirement or a certain point of success, money, savings, or relationships. Start experiencing it now, and stop accepting mediocrity. Instead, let's challenge it. Look for ways to innovate and get out of your comfort zone.

This is the season for me to launch a podcast in the coming months. I never thought I would be launching a podcast. I'm leaning into public speaking. I love to talk, yet it makes me very uncomfortable to talk in front of big groups of people. It is not within my comfort zone, but I know that's how I can reach more people and have a better impact.

Writing a book is innovative for me. I hated writing as a kid because I had to write in school, so I resisted it. I was made to write as a lawyer. I have resisted writing for so long, but embracing that I have a story to tell and that my story is valuable and important will help me impact that one life.

Ultimately, my vision is to create enough wealth within my ecosystem to fund a foundation that helps women and girls thrive in life. Thriving looks different for everyone. It is a whole-life perspective, from education to mentorship to health, well-being, spiritual growth, and more. I want to provide a resource that women and girls would need.

If a girl wants to take a yoga class because it will be good for her, I want to be able to say, "Yes, we have the resources for you." I want to say yes to people so they can start creating this beautiful life that I've been able to create.

That's what's front and center.

So how do I get there?

What path do I stumble, trip, skip, and dance along to get there?

That's what's driving me every day.

reframing pain & embracing change in motherhood

AIMEE GRECZMIEL

in /corporatemomcoach

corporatemomcoach.com

Aimee is a former Fortune 500 VP and Certified Life and Mindset Coach who helps working mothers manage their mental and emotional wellness and experience more balance, presence, and ease in their daily lives.

Aimee guides women to get clear on their desired outcomes so they may leave a lasting legacy for their families and make an impact in their careers. Aimee is an action-oriented mentor who has helped hundreds of individuals reach their goals while overcoming personal and professional challenges.

How do you define impact?

I love researching the origins of words and their meanings, so I looked up the dictionary's definition of "Impact," which is "to have a strong effect on someone or something."

How I define impact shows up in the work I do in my business. In fact, I created it out of a deep calling in my DNA once I became a mother. To me, I firmly believe that there's no bigger impact in life than the one a parent has with their child.

Society and culture often view impact mostly in terms of one's career or financial status, but I believe it is so much deeper than that. In today's society, so much time is spent intentionally growing one's career, but how often are people really focusing on the intentionality of their own growth? Becoming a mother is a MAJOR entry point for the inner work, and that is really the purpose behind what I do to support women in my business.

Looking back over your life, who has impacted you most, and what specific advice or guidance from them has not only influenced your personal growth but also significantly impacted the direction of your professional career?

Although we are shaped by many people and experiences in our lifetime, my family of origin has impacted me the most. More specifically, my parents and my Godmother have had the biggest impact simply because that's who I spent the most time with in my early life. Each of them provided me with what I would consider a useful model from which I can pull today.

For example, I pull from my mother's work ethic, commitment to her children, and a consistent reliance on her faith. When I became a mother myself, that's when I really began to wake up to the fact that I had this array of characteristics that I could access from my own childhood and previous experiences. It was an opportunity for me to evaluate what worked well, and what I could leave behind, and to really be intentional around the model I wanted to embody in my own motherhood experience.

From my father, I pull his grit, street smarts, and dedication to his children. Whether they realize it or not, my parents had this inherent belief centered around family, which involved self-sacrifice and supporting their children, almost to a fault. I don't know if this extreme was the right approach, but it taught me what true selflessness looks like, and that's a beautiful characteristic I am grateful for.

Lastly, my Godmother modeled career success. Growing up, she embodied this "I live the good life" attitude, and that's how she continues to live her life today. She always knew she was meant for goodness, that possibilities were endless, and abundance was always available, and I take a lot of that with me today.

————————

Think about the personal challenges you've overcome in your life. How did the obstacles that you've overcome play a part in the impact that you make now?

Challenges create resiliency, yet most people resist challenges, largely through complaining, which prolongs the unnecessary suffering and struggle associated with them. I was stuck in this space for a long time, particularly in my early adulthood.

There's a saying, "What we go through, we grow through," but most people get stuck in victimhood around their experiences and are too blind to see the lesson that the challenge is providing them. We live in a culture where it's even more important to reframe challenges into lessons so that we grow from them. When we do this, we reverse the narrative around challenges and create resiliency (as opposed to victimhood), which is then modeled for our children.

The thing is, no one is immune to challenges, yet we're all surprised whenever challenges occur as if life is supposed to be roses and rainbows 100% of the time.

So when we think about impact and its meaning of "having a strong effect on someone or something," it's important to remember that that definition goes both ways. A challenge can either have a positive impact or a negative impact.

Viewing a challenge as having a negative impact can keep us stuck in victimhood. However, viewing a challenge as a neutral impact, not even a positive impact, creates empowerment and choice.

When faced with challenges, we then have two choices. One is to decide if we will subscribe to the negative victimhood narrative or if we can meet ourselves from a more neutral position and ask, "What is the lesson here?"

Even in the coaching space, there's this concept called the 50/50 experience: 50% of the time, it's rainbows and roses, and 50% of the time, it's dark clouds and rain. This is what we experience in nature and the world around us.

When we become stuck in a challenge or when we "swirl" over a negative circumstance, we step into victimhood, and life suddenly isn't a 50/50 balance anymore. Now, it's more 80/20 because 80% of the time, we're stuck in victimhood, thinking about the problem and how it impacts us negatively, most of which are just stories that exist in our heads.

But when you adopt a more neutral mindset (again, not necessarily a positive mindset) around challenges, the sooner you can reassemble pieces into a different arrangement that serves you better. And what a gift to be able to reframe challenges in this way for ourselves and to model this for our children. In doing so, our children become more resilient and better primed to manage their own challenges throughout life.

Reflect on a moment in your professional life that you perceived as a failure. How did this experience lead to your most significant lessons of impact? Share how you have applied these lessons to positively influence your life and the lives of others.

I feel called to share more from my personal life, even though the question surrounds my professional life. The biggest challenge in my personal life that most would consider a failure was the divorce from my husband of 12 years and the father of my children. This was likely considered a failure by many in society. I even viewed it that way for a bit initially, but now my view on it is entirely different. The relationship and our marriage weren't a failure at all. The relationship was simply complete—it ran its course.

Even the word "divorce" carries so much baggage and is very triggering for people. But I've reframed it as something so much more empowering... divorce isn't really a split from a person, it's a divorce from your previous self.

We often forget that human beings are meant to evolve and grow. We are not meant to be stagnant, sedentary creatures, but we're meant to move forward physically, mentally, emotionally, and spiritually.

This concept alone—that situations, relationships, and moments are impermanent—has changed how I live my life and my overall worldview.

In spirituality, there's a universal law called the Law of Impermanence. It's a Buddhist concept that's a fundamental principle of nature that states that everything in existence is impermanent. This means that everything has a beginning, a middle, and an end. In Buddhism, it essentially means that nothing lasts forever, including our emotions, thoughts, and existence. There is a path to peace, but for that, you must embrace change rather than resist it.

This principle is similar to the saying, "The only constant is change," which is 100% true. I teach and embody this concept in my own life, to my clients, and to my children, because I firmly believe that embracing it can help people move through life's challenges more quickly.

Whether that's physically moving to a new location or changing your job, friends, or marital status, whatever it is... these are all patterns of growth, yet there's so much baggage with the relationship part and around marriage as a whole.

I still support marriage. It's a beautiful and wonderful thing for people to be together for a lifetime. But if it doesn't support their spiritual path, then perhaps the relationship is complete, and it's time to move on.

When I embraced that narrative and looked at it differently, it helped me view this perceived "failure" in life as an evolution to my new self and chapter.

How do you ensure your business practices align with ethical and sustainable principles while balancing profitability with making a positive impact?

In the coaching space, I see a lot of two things: toxic positivity and spiritual bypassing. Toxic positivity is the mindset of, "*Oh, just think differently. Change your mindset, and then your reality will change. Just shift your thoughts, and all will be happy and good.*" Spiritual bypassing occurs when one wants a desired outcome, but is unwilling to do uncomfortable inner work or go through the healing process to get to the other side of their pain. These two themes are very prominent in consumer spirituality, but on a large scale, **they generally don't work.**

They work for small, little tasks like taking out the trash or emptying the dishwasher, because no one is ever really excited to do that. For example, if you shift your mindset and think about your grandmother in the 1950s who had eight kids and no dishwasher, you realize it may not be so bad because you actually have this amazing appliance in your home. So positive psychology can work for little things like that, but for big life things, which is really what people come to coaching for, it just doesn't work.

What I teach and practice in my business is acknowledging that challenges and setbacks exist, and they are painful. The inner work isn't easy, and growth is uncomfortable. I guide my clients and help them reframe their thinking around loss, disappointment, frustration, and stress, not to make it go away or disappear, but to dig deeper and understand it better so that they can lead more fulfilling lives.

The pain we go through is purposeful, but often, we aren't taught how to process that pain. Instead, we're taught how to avoid loss. There's a difference, and you must feel it to heal it.

What role do partnerships and collaborations play in amplifying the impact of your business? How do you identify and cultivate meaningful relationships with other business leaders?

There are two ways to achieve success: there's a way through competition, and there's a way through collaboration. Culturally, we often think that the only way we can get ahead is if we compete and push other people down or climb the ladder and outperform everyone else.

In reality, the most authentic success can be achieved through collaboration because we're always in exchange with others. You simply cannot grow a business alone. You need other human beings to bounce ideas off of, challenge you, and partner with you, not from a financial standpoint of "What's in it for me?", but more from a reciprocity standpoint of "I help you, you help me, and we support each other." Everyone rises. It's like the quote, "If you want to go fast, go alone. If you want to go far, go together."

You can't run a successful business without partnerships and collaborations. They're essential.

In my business, partnerships and collaborations have come up for me fairly organically, and I allow them in intuitively. Simply by noticing if there's someone I need to have a conversation with or a nudge to follow up with someone who I just met at a conference. I've also been in several masterminds, where a handful of women just naturally connected, and we continue to talk and set up monthly touch bases. It's similar to making friendships and meeting people in your community. You can be intentional about it, but you can also just be open to receiving it organically.

———

Looking ahead, what are your aspirations for the future impact of your business, and how do you plan to continue evolving and innovating in this area?

As it relates to my future, I first need to briefly address my past.

The big turning point for me 100% was when I became a mother in 2016. My worldview changed drastically the moment I became a parent. Since then, I have become deeply committed to my own growth and healing.

Having my daughter in 2016 was the entry point to my awakening. I know it's not obvious to every woman, but it's available to all if you're open enough to see it. It wasn't an easy path. As I said, growth is uncomfortable, and the inner work isn't always easy, but I firmly believe that the greatest gift we can give to our loved ones is our own personal growth.

AT THE END OF THE DAY, WE'RE EACH RESPONSIBLE FOR OUR OWN WELL-BEING AND HEALING.

I also want to be very clear about the term "healing" or "inner work" and what that means because *no one* is immune to this. We all have two parts of us. In one aspect, we're all inherently good and divine, but in this other human aspect, we're all wounded and have scars.

We all have trauma. Trauma doesn't mean just getting hit by a car or having something awful happen to you as a child. It's our responsibility to find the balance between the two—between this inherent goodness and this wounding—to ensure that our wounds and fears don't overpower our inherent goodness.

So, we must remove the mask, put our egos in check, and raise awareness on how to process emotions and move through challenges in a way that isn't so devastating.

At the end of the day, we're each responsible for our own well-being and healing. My mission is to help mothers embrace that for themselves, their children, and the future generations in which they impact.

from heartache to homecoming

BUILDING A LEGACY OF FAMILY MEMORIES

CHELSEA LARSEN

in /chelsrae

mountainmoodstays.com

Chelsea lives for her family, to travel, see new places, and meet new people. Her career in mortgage lending led her to love all things sales, service, and real estate. She started investing in real estate to provide quality, safe homes for families to rent and build beautiful lives there. She dipped her toes into investing in vacation rentals by purchasing a mountain lake home and a beach condo that were meant to be second homes. She and her husband wanted to subsidize the expenses by renting out their vacation homes when they weren't enjoying them.

She fell in love with the hospitality side and providing amazing experiences to families. This realization led to the birth of Mountain Mood Stays, a luxury vacation rental management company. It was the perfect marriage of her passions: bringing families together, real estate investing, and travel. Through Mountain Mood Stays, she helps vacation homeowners rent their beloved homes while delivering stellar, elevated experiences to guests.

How do you define impact?

For me, impact is about having a positive imprint on someone else's life. It's about influencing others for good, spreading joy, serving, and adding value to their lives. In the context of Mountain Mood Stays, this translates to focusing on the person in front of me— our guests.

We strive to delight and surprise at every turn. Beyond providing gorgeous decor, comfortable beds, and clean houses, we focus on the little extras that make a stay memorable. For families, this means stocking our homes with board games, pack 'n' plays, and free beachwear. We offer early check-ins whenever possible, always aiming to elevate the guest experience.

This approach not only creates happy guests but also results in organic growth through word-of-mouth recommendations. People share their positive experiences with friends, family, and colleagues, attracting more guests who value the kind of experience we offer.

Looking back over your life, who has impacted you most, and what specific advice or guidance from them has not only influenced your personal growth but also significantly impacted the direction of your professional career?

My older brother, Jeremiah, is six years older than me. He's the most humble person. He is also extremely hardworking and solution-oriented. I could think of many obstacles to a goal, and he wouldn't even think they were obstacles. He just thinks, "What's the issue I have right now? How do I overcome it?" He doesn't get stuck in a place of "Oh, woe is me… Life is hard…" He simply overcomes.

When we were little kids and had to eat dinner at the dinner table, we hated Brussels sprouts. My sister loved them. We would pass them to my sister to eat the Brussels sprouts. Jer would be the older brother, stern and saying, "That is not okay. You need your nutrition. You need to eat these, just do it. They're gross, but you do it anyway." That's how he lives his life.

As I go through life and have challenges that present themselves, Jer comes to my mind. I find myself checking, *"How would Jer think about this? What would Jer do? How would he feel about me doing this? Would he be proud of me?"* And I've made my decisions based on that.

Jer affected the direction of my career by being an example of committing to finding ways to accomplish goals even when they were hard. Because of his example, I never felt that I couldn't do anything I wanted to. To meet my goals, I need to make a plan, and if something seems too hard to achieve, all that needs to happen is to find a way to overcome it.

He fueled my belief that anything is possible through hard work and creative thinking.

———————

Think about the personal challenges you've overcome in your life. How did the obstacles that you've overcome play a part in the impact that you make now?

I have anxiety and, at times, get stuck in moments of depression. On those rare darkest days, I find living fully and being present difficult.

My first experience with major depression was when my older sister gave up her rights to her children.

It was like a death in the family. I lost my nephews. They were around four and two years old. They were my whole world. When I was in high school, I would come home from school and be their caretaker, the equivalent of a nanny, but I was their aunt. I was in their world nonstop.

Then, one day, they were gone with no explanation. We didn't get to say goodbye. She signed her rights away and hadn't told anyone it was going to happen, and we never found out why. The last day I saw them, we had been playing in the living room, having a blast. My sister came to pick them up like it was a typical day... I never saw them again. It was heartbreaking, and I felt despair.

And it was extremely hard to overcome.

I didn't understand why the day-to-day of life, the world moving forward, continued as though I hadn't lost the two little boys who lit up my world with their sweet smiles, silly personalities, and tender cuddles. Didn't it know that I needed a pause?

I didn't like hurting and suffering. I wanted to live. I wanted to feel happy again... but I was in so much pain. I needed to change my mindset so that I could enjoy living again. I started intentionally connecting with people to pull myself out of my shell.

As I spent time with others and paid more attention to them, I noticed that we all experience pain. We all have really hard things to deal with, and life doesn't stop even when we're hurting.

I had assumed my friends and family were all happy, and I was the only one who wasn't. That wasn't the truth, I saw that we live full lives by finding joy in the darkness.

MINDSET WAS THE KEY.

It became apparent that I could still have joy amidst hardship because I had real-life examples of my friends and family doing it. They were finding pockets of happiness, while they experienced hard moments mixed in as well.

Mindset was the key.

Finding things to be grateful for, serving others, and telling myself positive stories helped me a lot, and they still continue to do so today.

On days that life feels extra heavy and seems impossible to function, I tell myself:

"All you have to do right now is the next right thing."

This simple thought has a huge impact and encourages me.

Losing my nephews made it even more important to make sure I spent as much time with my family as possible and build memories with them. A really sad event led to a beautiful core value of mine, and I have been able to go on many trips with my family, do amazing things, and make the coolest memories. I love that through hosting vacation home rentals, we get to bring families together and help them bond as well.

———————

Reflect on a moment in your professional life that you perceived as a failure. How did this experience lead to your most significant lessons of impact? Share how you have applied these lessons to positively influence your life and the lives of others.

My journey hasn't been without its challenges. Early in my career as a mortgage loan officer, I struggled with follow-up and time management. One particularly patient client, after waiting too long to hear back from me, finally lost his cool. He mockingly laughed and said, "I wish you the best in your career, but you're going nowhere."

That stinging criticism ignited a competitive drive in me. I was determined to do better, to be better for the people I served. This experience led me to master systems and processes, allowing me to be more present and deliver outstanding service consistently.

I now see this negative experience as a blessing in disguise. It pushed me beyond being merely "good enough" and inspired me to strive for excellence in everything I do.

How do you ensure your business practices align with ethical and sustainable principles while balancing profitability with making a positive impact?

The guiding principle that always works for me is focusing on the person in front of me.

If you're focused on them, you're always going to do the right thing. While hosting short-term rentals, I'm focused on the experience. They want to stay in our homes and can stay anywhere. What are we doing to delight and surprise them and deliver an elevated experience? We want to give them elevated experiences. At the basic level, that's having gorgeous decor, comfortable beds and pillows, and a clean house—fully stocked with extra touches.

We focus heavily on families. We want families to come into our homes and give them time together to build lasting memories. We put in board games, pack 'n' plays, free beachwear, etc., in our homes, giving them all these little extras. Whenever we can, we do early check-ins. Our goal is to delight and surprise. Elevating their experience comes from focusing on what's best for them.

> *I learn the most by observing other people and focusing on what's best for the person I'm serving.*

When you serve with others at the heart of your actions, you gain an unintended benefit—free marketing. People will share their positive experiences with friends, family, business partners, and coworkers. The word-of-mouth promotion attracts more clients who want to work with you, leading to free referrals and business growth.

*What role do partnerships and collaborations
play in amplifying the impact of your business?
How do you identify and cultivate meaningful
relationships with other business leaders?*

It's important to build relationships and add value to
those people. For example, I remember things that
are important to them. If I see something I can help
them with or point out, I will forward it to them.

*Think of how you can help somebody else, and
do it—you will get the same in return.*

It's important to continue nurturing the relationships,
too. Don't only talk business but also check in on
a personal level. The idea is that you're lifting each
other up to reach your goals. You can have really
fun friendships and partner together while helping
to lift each other up. That could be collaboration on
podcasts or sharing ideas on how you can help them
elevate their business or establish their branding.

Partnership and collaboration to build your business,
outside transactional relationships and referrals, are
very significant. Making great friends while helping
each other in our businesses is the icing on the cake.

Looking ahead, what are your aspirations for the future impact of your business, and how do you plan to continue evolving and innovating in this area?

As I look to the future, my aspirations for Mountain Mood Stays continue to evolve. The challenges our world faces, particularly the impact of wars on families and children, have deeply affected me. As a mother of two young children, the idea of families being torn apart and children suffering is heartbreaking.

These thoughts have led me to a powerful question: "How could we help raise children to want to be a positive force in the world and take action to do so?" While we can't single-handedly stop wars, we can spread kindness and inspire others to do the same.

My vision is to expand Mountain Mood Stays to include family vacation retreats where we would curate trips, explore destinations, and combine fun experiences with cultural immersion and community service.

When we travel and experience other cultures, the people who live where we are visiting, and immerse ourselves in their world, it bridges a gap between our world and theirs. It helps us love them more, have empathy for their challenges, and highlight how we really aren't that different from each other. We want to be safe and loved, be with family and friends, and eat delicious food.

The goal is to raise curious souls who learn about others, serve, and spread joy.

By bringing families together to experience different cultures and give back to communities, we can foster empathy, understanding, and a desire to make a positive impact.

I believe that love can beget love, and through travel and meaningful experiences, we can bridge gaps between cultures and foster a more compassionate world.

It's our obligation, as a society, to be a force for good.

"YOU NEVER KNOW WHEN A THOUGHT
IN YOUR HEAD THAT YOU DIDN'T PUT
OUT WAS ACTUALLY THE THOUGHT THAT
WOULD CHANGE THE WORLD."

Unknown

the value of
inclusive connection

JEAN HANSEN

in /jean-marie-hansen

pathwaysinlife.com

As the founder of Pathways in Life, Jean Hansen works with entrepreneurs and parents of children with special needs to create a game plan for the unexpected, bringing peace of mind and allowing them to focus on living fully instead of worrying about the unknown. Jean has watched dear friends and close family members face sudden and overwhelming medical crises, untimely deaths, and other highly stressful situations. It became clear to her that many people are unprepared to handle these hardships. That is why she decided to start her own business, to coach others to plan for and navigate these difficult circumstances.

With a 25-year background in education, coaching, and working with Special Olympics, Jean brings a wealth of experience to her coaching practice. She understands the challenges of family dynamics and draws on her own experiences to guide others in creating a plan for the future. Jean serves as a personal life strategist, helping clients formulate and implement strategies to navigate life's journey. Jean is a best-selling author and hosts a weekly podcast, The Jean Hansen Show, where she unveils stories of how people have overcome challenges and redefined limits.

In her spare time, she can be found sailing, golfing, hiking, and spending time with her two children, Tanner and Elizabeth, and their beloved family dog, Apollo. Jean is passionate about supporting others in planning for the unexpected and embracing the journey ahead, empowering individuals to shape their own paths.

———————

How do you define impact?

"A grain of rice can tip the scale."
–Unknown

Impact is all the little things we do that can change somebody's life. We may or may not know the effect that we have had. Little things like opening a door for somebody, giving someone a smile, hug, or recognition when they've done great work can impact somebody's life.

There's a ripple effect when you drop a pebble on a pond. Hopefully, the impact I'm making on somebody's life will allow them space to impact other people's lives as well.

Impact can be little or big, and it can also be positive or negative.

I strive to create a positive impact and change people's lives. My big mission in life is to see, value, respect, and include others. I hope that's always positive, but there are probably times in my life when I have done something negative or created a negative impact. It's important to recognize that, make amends, apologize, and learn from it.

When my son, Tanner, was younger, I realized that I didn't always respond in a way that I wish I had. It's one of those things you realize as a parent: you can't change the past, but you learn and move on. I had a conversation with him about how I felt, and it wasn't easy. I told him I was so sorry that I wasn't more present and more patient then, and that I wasn't seeing things then as I do now. I didn't pay attention to him at times when he may have needed me, and I wanted to acknowledge that and share that I really "see" him now. That's an example of impact. I recognized that I didn't parent the way I wanted to, but I was able to learn, do better, and change. It's an ever-evolving process where we're hopefully constantly growing and improving.

Looking back over your life, who has impacted you most, and what specific advice or guidance from them has not only influenced your personal growth but also significantly impacted the direction of your professional career?

The first person that came to my mind was my mom. Then, when I really thought about it, my sister Angela came to mind. Angela was born when I was five, and she was the fifth of seven children. My mom always felt that there was something different about Angela and that she was not developing the same as the other kids. The doctors kept saying that not all children talk, learn, or walk at the same time. My mom kept pushing back and saying she knew something wasn't right with Angela. Around age 2 or 3, the doctors finally did some testing and found out that she had an intellectual disability.

I remember when she was growing up, she didn't always have the words. She would get really angry, scream, and get so frustrated. Being a parent now, I can understand the frustration if you don't have any words to express your feelings.

Angela and I were always really close and connected. I spent a lot of time in middle school and high school volunteering in her classroom or working with her at camps. When it came time to pick a profession, I always knew I wanted to be a teacher. I went to college, and I thought I wanted to be a special education teacher, so I went into teaching and got a degree in education. Getting a license in Special Education required me to go back to school and get a master's degree. I got a teaching job and I realized it wasn't quite what I thought it would be. While I enjoyed teaching, I learned that I enjoyed working with adults and creating a curriculum.

In high school, I volunteered and coached Angela in Special Olympics basketball and swimming. When a job opened up, I applied for it. That led me to work with adults, creating curriculum, teaching, and training. Throughout my career, I have also worked with schools to create more inclusive environments where special ed and general ed students can come together in sports, leadership, and advocacy.

I love my work because I can see its impact and how it changes people's lives. It helps people accept others for their differences and create meaningful friendships. When we were growing up, there were a couple of times when people would make fun of my sister, and she would laugh, not knowing that they were making fun of her. I was so frustrated and angry. It comes full circle to see students now accepting others and not laughing at each other but with each other, showing true joy and friendship. It's because of Angela that I've gained those experiences. She's impacted my life in that way.

My brother and I are also the trustees of my parents' trust. During COVID, we met with the attorney to update everything. A long time ago, they put a trust together for Angela because they wanted to ensure that she was always taken care of when anything happened to them. When we went through that process, I realized that there were all kinds of additional details to deal with that weren't in their estate plan. Information like passwords, medical information, banking, and insurance. All of this information wasn't in one place, and I had no idea how to access it if something happened to Mom and Dad, and they couldn't tell me. That's what led me to create my business so that people can think through and talk about those details in a way that's not overwhelming or stressful. Having a plan in place can allow you to enjoy life and not have to worry when something unexpected does happen.

Angela has brought me to so many different places in my life. I am so thankful and appreciative that she's a part of our family. Our whole family realizes that blessing. She is so joyful and reminds me to enjoy things and that they don't have to be complicated.

Think about the personal challenges you've overcome in your life. How did the obstacles that you've overcome play a part in the impact that you make now?

Probably the biggest obstacle I've overcome is accepting myself for truly being who I am. When I was in my 20s, I realized that I was gay, and I didn't want to be. I didn't want to accept it. I kept thinking it was a phase. In my late 20s and early 30s, I realized it was *who I am*.

I have a large family, and I was so afraid of coming out and telling people. One by one, I told my siblings. It's the hardest thing to put yourself in that situation where, on the one hand, you need to share it because you can't hide it anymore, but I also knew that I was taking a chance of not being accepted. It was one of the biggest struggles to go through. I'm so close with my siblings, but each time it was hard. They were all so accepting of me. They were like, "Duh. We knew." Still, the hardest thing was to decide to tell my parents.

When I was 30, I decided to take time off work, travel around the United States, and see things. I didn't have a plan except to see as much as I could, and it felt empowering. Right before I was planning to leave, there was an initiative on the Oregon ballot that was telling governments and local agencies that you can't promote, encourage, or even acknowledge homosexuality. I was reading through all the voter pamphlets, and it was horrifying the things that they were portraying about people who are gay. It said we were awful to children, that we were pedophiles and all sorts of other horrible things that were so hurtful and not true. I sat and cried because that was not me. I wasn't that person. As scared as I was to tell my parents, I realized that in telling them, they would know who I truly was. I also wanted to stand up and say that we are not what was being described in the voter's pamphlet.

I wanted to tell them we live in society and are regular people who do things like everybody else. I knew it wouldn't be easy, but I called my parents and said I needed to come for a visit and wanted to have a conversation. I told them I wasn't sick or pregnant and that I didn't need money. When I was with them to have the conversation, it was the hardest three words to get out of my mouth. We were making dinner in the kitchen, and they asked me what I wanted to talk to them about. In a squeaky voice, I blurted out, "I'm gay," followed by a ton of tears. I didn't know what to expect. It felt like forever, but then they put their arms around me, hugged me, and we cried.

It was the first time that I've ever felt that depth of unconditional love.

Coming out to them, I realized that my family accepted me for who I am. Even if nobody else does, I have them in my corner. That made me realize that everybody has parts of themselves that they might not want to accept. But for me, I realized I'm a good person, and I have a lot of things to do in life. It made me feel comfortable in knowing who I am.

We're all constantly growing, changing, and learning, but I felt I didn't have to hide anymore. That was probably the biggest thing for me to accept and overcome, but feeling unconditional love from family and friends was incredible. You know it in your head, but sometimes you question it. I kept telling myself, "Of course they love me," but I felt it in my heart after sharing and telling people.

———————

Reflect on a moment in your professional life that you perceived as a failure. How did this experience lead to your most significant lessons of impact? Share how you have applied these lessons to positively influence your life and the lives of others.

Overall, I feel like I've had so much success in my career, but there was a time in 2007 when I did a pivot. I went to work with my sister in the mortgage industry, went through the whole process, became a mortgage broker, and started working with clients.

In 2008, people asked us why I was going into the mortgage business because a recession was coming. I'm a positive person, so I thought everything would be fine. Of course, later in 2008, a financial crisis did come. Suddenly, I thought it probably wasn't the best decision, but I was still determined to make it work. But reality hit, and I decided it wasn't the time to become a mortgage broker because the whole financial landscape was changing rapidly.

One thing I learned from that experience was that I'm pretty persistent. Once I set my mind to something, I will do whatever I can to make it work. I also realized that I really enjoy connecting with people, but connecting with people around mortgages wasn't really my thing. I took that lesson to realize that my purpose in life is connecting, teaching, and reaching out to people. I went back to Special Olympics and started working with schools educating and promoting inclusion.

Realizing my talent for connecting with people and teaching has fueled my growth in my new business. Seeing people light up because of the connections I can make with them keeps my cup full and overflowing. It also reiterated to me that there are many different ways to make money.

Of course, we all need to make money, but there is truth in the saying, "Do what you love, and the money will follow."

How do you ensure your business practices align with ethical and sustainable principles while balancing profitability with making a positive impact?

When people work with me, I want them to know they can trust me. I often find myself in vulnerable conversations with people discussing sensitive topics. I have a responsibility to help manage, hold, and know that when people confide in me, it will stay there. I'm not going to do anything to jeopardize that trust. I want people to see that I'm here to help and do something for them and add value.

As I grow my business, I want to give back. When people choose me, I hope they know what's important to me and that everything I give back aligns with who I am.

Looking ahead, what are your aspirations for the future impact of your business, and how do you plan to continue evolving and innovating in this area?

The ripple of impact is a theme here. One of the things I realized is that while we're discussing having a plan for unexpected events that might happen in life, there's also an opportunity for people to realize that you can do, be, or have anything you want. During these conversations, I find it allows them to take inventory of where they've been and where they want to go. Sometimes, that sounds trite, but if you're in a place you're not happy in or not doing something you really want to do, you can change that. Through some of the conversations, I hope people will come to that realization. I want them to see this as an opportunity and a stepping stone to achieving their goal, and we'll start working on it a little bit more.

Another aspiration is to help my daughter. I adopted her from Guatemala, and she wants to create a business and go back and do more to help the women in her country. I love being able to see her and support her in those ways as she learns how to start and grow a business, helping her so that she can create more impact.

I've also come to the realization that we all have challenges that happen in our lives. Some of them are behind us that we look back on, and some are still ahead of us. But challenges don't have to define us—especially if we can take the time to connect with people we love and have the conversations that empower us to get through the struggle or the obstacle. Taking this step can lead to more freedom, allowing us to focus on living all out, what that means, and what that might look like. If you realize that it's time to make a change because you want to make an impact in a different way, there are so many people willing and able to help you.

I'm hoping that, in some small way, I might be the person, that grain of rice, that tips the scale so people make those realizations to live fully, and make whatever impact they desire in life.

*transforming a male-dominated
industry through female leadership*

STACIA HOBSON

in /staciahobson
imageindustries.com

Stacia is the co-owner of Image Industries, Inc., and she began her career in the family business upon graduating from college. Although her plan was never to work for the business, let alone own it, she was the key driver in transforming it from 100% distribution to 100% manufacturing.

Today, she runs operations for her family's multimillion-dollar manufacturing business, serving nine district vertical markets. Learning to navigate the "family politics" provided a sturdy foundation for future growth.

Stacia is acutely aware of what it takes to succeed as a woman in a male-dominated blue-collar industry. She is passionate and proud to be in the manufacturing industry, as she feels it's the backbone of the United States. With over three decades of experience under her belt, she has acquired extensive practical knowledge of business relationships and entrepreneurship.

Stacia is employing her vast experience to provide business consulting services to guide leaders of all sizes of businesses to embrace the bold decision-making needed to achieve massive transformation. Her expertise lies in unlocking new possibilities while helping clients navigate the risks associated with these courageous choices. She leads by example and leans on her experience, as she herself has had to make many daring decisions. She aims to create a ripple effect by encouraging individuals and organizations to fearlessly pursue their ambitions. By instilling a sense of empowerment and self-belief, she encourages her clients to envision and achieve what they once perceived as just brave goals.

―――――

How do you define impact?

Impact can have many meanings that will change and develop throughout the course of your life. Today, I define it quite differently than I did just five years ago.

I now have 58 employees. When I moved out of Illinois, I had 44. At that time, I didn't realize how significant of an impact I would have on this community. I am now providing jobs for people who want them in an economically deprived area where the poverty level sits at 70%. Needless to say, the community here is very different from the one I left in Illinois.

While jobs are important to everybody, the people within this community view those jobs at a very different level than what most of America experiences. These jobs are essential for survival. Our business was recruited by Mississippi's Delta Strong and Coahoma county's Economic Development to provide 50 jobs in exchange for grants and tax incentives that would substantially impact our company's growth. It was later told to me that those 50 jobs would positively affect 30,000 people, so to me, that's impact!

Now, I'm helping my team members, training them, leveling them up, and teaching them new skills. This provides them the freedom of choice to stay with us or to leave with new skills that will help them get other jobs at decent wages, allowing them to continue to put food on their table.

––––––––––––

Think about the personal challenges you've overcome in your life. How did the obstacles that you've overcome play a part in the impact that you make now?

Being a young female in a male-dominated industry has had many challenges. I joined the business world in 1987 at the age of 22. Chauvinism was very alive and well and considered to be a good and healthy practice. Learning to successfully navigate those early experiences of being looked down upon and spoken to poorly shaped me and made me tough.

I didn't realize until very recently how direct I am in my communication with people. Part of that is thinking to myself: "*Alright. You are a female, and you need to get things done. You need to take charge.*" Part of taking charge is having that masculine energy that says, "This is what needs to happen, and you, who I hired to do this job, need to make it happen." I try not to micromanage. I try to give people the job, take the reins, and go with it, but it comes with a lot of responsibility on both my part and theirs to ensure they do just that.

There's a fine line between coaching and leadership that will enable your team to be successful. As women, we tend to be too compassionate. You need to be compassionate in an environment and line of business such as mine, but compassion may often be confused with weakness. I've learned that communication needs to be clear and measured, but direct to get the desired results. Sometimes, it is not well received, but it is what it is... otherwise, we wouldn't achieve the desired outcome.

I've worked in all areas of business and can attest to the fact there's still plenty of chauvinism today. While it is much better in the younger generations, it still exists.

Reflect on a moment in your professional life that you perceived as a failure. How did this experience lead to your most significant lessons of impact? Share how you have applied these lessons to positively influence your life and the lives of others.

Progress is built on failure.

I've encountered my fair share. One was promoting women on my plant floor and not recognizing, even though I'm a female, their challenges of being promoted. In my vast years of experience, it is unusual for a female on the plant floor to want to be promoted into a leadership position such as team lead or middle management. When I find talent and try to promote it, the females really struggle. I've had two failures, and I am on my third try. In my second failure, I started to notice some similarities where I made mistakes.

I've learned that men on the plant floor are straightforward to promote. They may not be confident because they have to learn a new skill set, but men take that leadership role much more straightforwardly than women. I have a new team lead, and she's fabulous. She's knocking it out of the park. I have given her a lot more mentorship, coaching, and validation. Her previous supervisor, who is male, has also jumped on that bandwagon to help her become successful. Because we provided feedback, coaching, and inspiration on a daily basis and told her she was doing a good job, she developed a new mindset. She's no longer a team member but a team lead, and that's a new identity for her. Previously, I did not recognize that this is a new identity that these women are taking on. Nor did I fully understand that part of a new identity was a mindset shift. Silly, I know, as I have had multiple mindset and identity shifts myself—but it was business—had to perform or else.

Men don't have that. They are much more confident at first, even if it takes time to learn new skills and processes. Women just aren't that way. My dad had a sink-or-swim approach, and he indoctrinated me with that mindset, "I think I can do this, so therefore I can do this." But oftentimes, women are not taught this approach and struggle to adapt to this new mindset.

I am grateful that I've identified this key issue that contributed to these failures and have turned that learning experience into something positive for someone else.

How do you ensure your business practices align with ethical and sustainable principles while balancing profitability with making a positive impact?

You keep your promises. You pay your bills. You negotiate a fair price. You talk with your employees and suppliers to address issues. You work things out. There's all this focus on ethics, but it's really not that hard. Just do the right thing. If you have values and live by them as a human being, your business will be fine. You don't have to have slave labor to make money.

I've never regretted doing the right thing. You never regret that. I've lost sleep over many topics, but doing the right thing isn't one of them.

What role do partnerships and collaborations play in amplifying the impact of your business? How do you identify and cultivate meaningful relationships with other business leaders?

Business, like all of life, is about relationships. As a business owner and leader, you have to be prepared to talk with people in their language in the way they need to hear it.

I talked before about being too direct, and that is true. I know am that way with people. However, I always circle back to them and ask them how they are doing, how their family is, or how their weekend went.

ALWAYS BRING THE CONVERSATION BACK TO THE RELATIONSHIP.

Always bring the conversation back to the relationship.

It's equally important to have non-business conversations with team members, whether they're team leads, production supervisors, or laborers. Those conversations go miles to forming a bond between everyone in your company. It's a good feeling when your boss doesn't just care about your scrap numbers and asks about your weekend or family. It's about showing people that they mean more than just a number.

As far as working with other leaders, I love building rapport and relationships and networking with other leaders. You learn so much because we all think so differently. We're humans, and it's incredible how we have the same experience and walk away with a completely different definition of that experience. It's fascinating, and I always walk away with more "tools" in my toolbox!

When I talk to male manufacturing leaders versus female manufacturing leaders, their take on outcomes or situations is often very different. It's very interesting because one's not right and one's not wrong. It's eye-opening how people interpret things, but building those relationships is imperative. The kind of network where you can call others to obtain their advice becomes your village.

———————

Looking ahead, what are your aspirations for the future impact of your business, and how do you plan to continue evolving and innovating in this area?

This is a twofold answer. One for the manufacturing business and one for the proverbial "side hustle."

For the manufacturing business, I am working heavily with the community and other leaders to build a program to help high school children get out of the scheme of poverty. It's an elaborate program. It will take Herculean efforts to get it off the ground, and it's not something that just happens overnight. We have to educate and identify a pathway for these kids to follow and execute. Further, the employer has to be on board with the whole plan.

In a recent meeting with the community stakeholders, we determined that these kids require mentorship at many levels. Without that, any growth or movement toward lowering the poverty line here is not sustainable. I recently had a conversation with the local Workforce Development Community College and communicated that we are in desperate need of a mentorship program—not just for our business, but for the community as a whole.

They wholeheartedly agreed, and we are now in the early stages of creating a mentorship program that incorporates the town and county government to help people of all ages, not just kids, because we all struggle. Many of the residents simply don't have a sound support system to assist them through their situation. I recognize that I'm not the person to have those conversations because I am their boss. I am the business owner. Having those conversations may be considered manipulative and potentially frowned upon, so I need to shore that up. What I do know is that employing the buddy system provides great benefits to people who are either new or struggling with their jobs. Having a peer working with others may be the key to success here. When they get a buddy who can help them, even if it's just listening, there is a marked improvement in their attitude.

As for my side hustle, business consulting, I am looking at creating a space for business owners to develop thoughts and explore big dreams. I help entrepreneurs turn their big dreams into targets and develop strategies to aggressively go after them. I find it fascinating that people are afraid of saying yes to opportunities. Even if the larger goal does not develop in the near term, there is a great benefit to simply having a conversation and potentially meeting other people! Saying yes opens up so many doors, and it's your choice. It's not a commitment, but simply saying yes to new ideas and new mindsets and holding space for the opportunity for both personal and professional development.

unmasking authenticity

ILLUMINATING THE PATH
TO IMPACTFUL BRANDS

LOUISE TAYLOR

in /louisemctaylor

fireflyeffect.ca

For over two decades, Louise Taylor navigated the intricate world of brand and marketing leadership. Her journey spans from corporate giants to purpose-driven organizations, all rooted in her early days of creative entrepreneurship. As founder of Firefly Effect, she serves as fractional Chief Marketing and Brand Officer, blending strategic insight with heartfelt creativity to transform brands and champion exceptional customer experiences.

As a Fascinate Certified Advisor and High Sensory Coach, she taps into the nuanced aspects of human connection and brand perception.

She believes each business has a heartbeat, and her role is to help that pulse be felt by others. It's not just about marketing tactics; it's about understanding and sharing the human stories behind every brand.

How do you define impact?

Impact is the legacy that we leave.

It is the knowledge, stories, and lessons that I've acquired over the years. It's about sharing those and paying it forward so that future generations can learn and grow from the experience and interaction they've had with me.

Impact means the freedom and alignment that come from shedding my facade and living authentically. When we share our whole selves, we move from a divided existence to one that multiplies joy and peace.

My parents taught me to always leave places better than I found them. This principle shapes my approach to life and business, underscoring that we always have the choice to positively influence others. I've embraced the philosophy that impact comes from vulnerability.

Brené Brown's words ring true: *"There is no courage without vulnerability."* This mantra has become central to my personal and professional ethos. Those who matter will value our openness, not judge it.

———

Looking back over your life, who has impacted you most, and what specific advice or guidance from them has not only influenced your personal growth but also significantly impacted the direction of your professional career?

Reflecting on my past, multiple negative experiences have profoundly influenced my path. While these stories are challenging to recount, they are integral to my journey and the support system I eventually found.

In high school, I had aspirations of becoming an architect, blending my love for creativity with my strengths in math and science. However, in my last year, a new teacher's inappropriate behavior made me so uncomfortable that I abandoned my dream, leading me to pursue art and design at a small college instead. This early betrayal of trust marked the beginning of a pattern that would haunt me for years.

My first summer job in college as a junior designer brought another harsh lesson. I'd landed a coveted role: a summer job in my field, guaranteed for three years. I pushed myself to get out of my introverted shell and deliver results. At the summer-end barbecue, my boss took me into the camera darkroom and exposed himself to me. Shocked and terrified, I ran from the office. I never told anyone and never returned for the remaining two years. Sadly, this incident was not isolated but part of a pattern of exploitation by men in power, which played out repeatedly over the next twenty years. Each instance further eroded my ability to trust others and myself.

To cope, I built an impenetrable facade: smile and excel professionally, but as a person, be invisible, and stay safe. I convinced myself that nothing phased me, that being invisible meant being protected. But deep down, I knew I was destined for more.

Positive Influences

Amidst these personal struggles, two pivotal experiences began to shift my perspective. In the first instance, I was invited to join my company's Women's Network, which supported women's professional development across 17 sub-businesses. For the first time, I felt the potent power of community support. Shortly after joining, I was asked to lead the Women's Network. The support I felt and the impact we had on women's lives in the organization inspired me.

In the second pivotal time, during my last corporate role, I reported to the Chief Information Officer, one of the few senior women in a male-dominated company and one of the few leaders in my career who saw me as a person, not just a means to deliver business results. She helped me learn to trust again.

These experiences helped me realize how crucial community connections are. They inspired me to dedicate myself to helping women entrepreneurs embrace their true selves.

And, it helped me in my journey of accepting and loving myself.

Think about the personal challenges you've overcome in your life. How did the obstacles that you've overcome play a part in the impact that you make now?

Growing up in an authoritarian home, I learned at a young age to suppress my feelings. I believed that invisibility kept me safe. I was wrong.

IT WAS TIME TO FIND MY VOICE, NOT JUST FOR MYSELF, BUT FOR MY DAUGHTERS.

In my early forties, as a recently divorced single mother of two young daughters, life forced me to confront my facade.

A grape-sized tumor growing in my jaw required extensive surgery. For the first time, I was forced to slow down, heal, and reflect on my life. Standing before the mirror, my jaw wired shut, I realized: that this happened *for* me, not *to* me.

It was time to find my voice, not just for myself, but for my daughters.

Yet, my journey was far from over. A few years later, while head of marketing at a large financial services company, I faced another health crisis. The initial surgery successfully removed an 8-pound tumor, but the pathology report revealed aggressive pre-cancer cells, necessitating a full hysterectomy just 4 weeks later. This surgery was complicated by a severe drop in blood pressure, and I nearly died, losing half my blood in a life-saving follow-up surgery.

In that precarious moment, my thoughts were consumed by my young daughters. As a single mother, I could not fathom leaving them without a parent. Surviving this ordeal solidified my determination to live fully and authentically.

These challenges taught me that our bodies store trauma and signaled me if I didn't address my feelings. Determined to take control of my life, I embraced vulnerability and authenticity, both personally and professionally. The journey to find my voice and speak my truth was not solely for me but also for my daughters. This path led me to support others in living truthfully, fostering deep connections and trust.

———————

How do you ensure your business practices align with ethical and sustainable principles while balancing profitability with making a positive impact?

My guiding principle, *'Illuminating Visions,'* shapes my approach to work. I choose to collaborate with organizations that care about their societal impact, not just profits. Working with purpose-driven clients, like a community-based credit union developing solutions to help struggling homeowners overcome financial hurdles, ensures my business practices align with ethical values while balancing profitability and positive impact.

For instance, partnering with a brain injury not-for-profit agency to reimagine their brand and expand their advocacy demonstrated my commitment to community and conscious marketing. I've also worked closely with pet care service providers to build brands that resonate with compassion and trust. These collaborations embody my dedication to transparency and genuine connection.

I believe in saying no to clients whose values don't align with mine. This leaves space for meaningful connections with those who genuinely care about their work's impact.

My commitment to conscious marketing principles and community support ensures my business practices align with my ethical values. It's about striking a balance: we can be profitable while also making a positive impact. In fact, I believe the two go hand in hand.

———————

What role do partnerships and collaborations play in amplifying the impact of your business? How do you identify and cultivate meaningful relationships with other business leaders?

Partnerships and collaborations are pivotal in amplifying my business's impact. I used to think I could do it all alone. However, I realized that working with others creates richer solutions and experiences, fostering innovation and growth.

As a corporate marketing leader in my previous role, I built a marketing team from the ground up in a sales-focused company. It wasn't easy! Initially, the organization didn't understand the value of marketing. However, my resilience and determination paid off, and by the time I left, I had established Marketing as a strategic partner supporting all business lines. This transformation wouldn't have been possible without collaboration. I believed in the importance of empowering rather than controlling people, listening to their ideas, supporting their growth, and bringing out the best in my teams.

Building relationships with CEOs and business leaders, providing honest and informed insights, and making difficult decisions when necessary are integral to my practice. When forming a collaborative team, I look for individuals with complementary skills and shared values. Evolution is essential, and re-evaluating needs over time ensures continued alignment with our mission. As a highly sensitive person and an introvert, I find joy in deep, heartfelt conversations rather than small talk, making meaningful connections, and focusing on clients who share my values.

I embrace the philosophy of '**Givers Gain**,' from BNI, which holds that giving freely of your resources and support will eventually circle back to you. If I can help someone, I will, trusting that this positive energy will return in kind.

––––––––––––

Looking ahead, what are your aspirations for the future impact of your business, and how do you plan to continue evolving and innovating in this area?

When I smile today, it's no longer because I am wearing a mask, but because I'm genuinely happy. This journey from facade to authenticity has been transformative, both personally and professionally.

Having found joy from the inside out, I aim to help businesses and individuals shine with sincerity. Authenticity is at the core of a thriving brand. By embracing and expressing inner truths, brands can foster joy, richness, and abundance. This authenticity aligns internal values with external representations, creating a harmonious and powerful brand identity.

I incorporate creative channels like photography and painting into my work, telling richer, more personal stories. These artistic expressions add depth and dimension to brand narratives, making them more relatable and impactful. The Firefly Effect symbolizes igniting the inner glow within us, leading to collective brilliance. One firefly may light up a small area, but imagine a field of fireflies shining together, illuminating a path for themselves and others.

In my journey, I aim to help entrepreneurs and business leaders find their unique voice, equipping them with the knowledge and support to succeed authentically. Whether through individual engagements, community programs, or group settings, my goal is to build impactful brands that embody the true essence of their founders, maximizing impact and by fostering heartfelt connection.

Additionally, I continue to innovate and evolve my services to meet the changing needs of my clients. Beyond individual engagements, this includes offering workshops, online courses, and community-based programs that empower individuals and businesses to live and work authentically. I believe that continuous learning and adaptation are key to staying relevant and impactful in an ever-changing world.

Looking ahead, I aspire to deepen my impact by empowering more individuals and businesses to live and work authentically. I strive to light paths for others, fostering a world where authenticity breeds success and fulfillment. As Carl Jung wisely said, *"The privilege of a lifetime is to become who you truly are."*

My journey from personal struggles to professional triumphs has taught me the profound power of authenticity. Shedding my facade and embracing vulnerability has not only transformed my life but also enabled me to create meaningful and lasting impacts through my work. By helping others find and express their genuine selves, I aim to foster a world where businesses and individuals thrive in harmony with their true values.

In every challenge lies an opportunity for growth, and in every story, there is a lesson to be shared. My story is a testament to the power of resilience, community, and authenticity. It is a journey of transformation, not just for myself but for everyone I have the privilege of working with.

Together, we can create a brighter, more authentic future for all.

"ALONE, WE CAN DO SO LITTLE;
TOGETHER, WE CAN DO SO MUCH."

Helen Keller

beyond the borders

JUDY TIERNEY

in /tierneyjudy

judytierney.com

Judy Tierney is an Austin-based REALTOR®, real estate coach, investor, and world travel expert. After a long corporate career running her own marketing and communications firm, she's now inspiring multi-passionate, professional women like herself to build confidence and wealth through real estate investing and to live more purposeful and experience-filled lives.

A true Texan at heart, Judy is a graduate of Southern Methodist University and the University of Texas at Austin MBA program. She's lived everywhere from New Jersey to New York to San Francisco and has explored over 30 countries across all seven continents.

When she's not off on her next adventure, you'll find Judy enjoying time with family and friends, running along Lady Bird Lake, or soaking up Austin's live music scene.

How do you define impact?

Impact is about creating a lasting change
that contributes to a better future for people,
our communities, and, ideally, the world. It's a
transformation that continues to provide value
and make a difference long after you take the
initial action.

Each day, my intention is to make an impact in
several ways. In my real estate business, I help
professional women who are unsure about how to
start investing, overcome their fears and trepidation.
I love watching their confidence—and their bank
accounts—grow as they discover a new way to
accumulate wealth. It's not just about buying
property; it's about empowering them to achieve the
freedom and financial success to support and spend
more time with their families.

I also make an impact by encouraging people
to create experiences and memories with those
they love. Life is too short to fill our days only with
work and responsibilities. It brings me joy to see
so many of my real estate clients find a way to use
their investment properties or the money they
earn through rental income to make some of these
dreams come true.

STEPPING OUT OF OUR COMFORT ZONES CAN LEAD TO REMARKABLE PERSONAL GROWTH.

Whether it's welcoming people from around the world to their vacation homes, to paying off debt, to sending their children to private school, they are setting an example about what's possible and making an impression on the next generation.

Stepping out of our comfort zones can lead to remarkable personal growth.

So, whatever we do today—whether it's teaching someone the tricks to investing in real estate or encouraging someone to embark on an adventure—it doesn't just change them in the short term; it gives them the confidence to continue to turn small dreams into epic realities. And best of all, it inspires those around them to do the same.

Looking back over your life, who has impacted you most, and what specific advice or guidance from them has not only influenced your personal growth but also significantly impacted the direction of your professional career?

The people who have influenced my life the most are my parents. As working parents with six kids, they still managed to juggle all our activities, keep up the household, and wrangle everyone together for dinner each night—all without any outside help. Having grown up in the Depression era, they never took money or possessions for granted. They valued hard work and education, but they also had a passion for life and for having fun.

My parents passed on to me two key traits that have shaped me personally and professionally: my love of a wide range of interests and my relentless work ethic.

I don't recall a quiet moment in our house or a time I wasn't engaged in some activity. When we weren't at school or participating in our after-school commitments, our house was filled with friends, books, games, and creative projects. Each summer, the entire family piled into our station wagon for summer road trips across the U.S. When I was the last kid at home, as a sophomore in high school, my parents took me on my first international trip to

London, an adventure that sparked my obsession and passion for traveling and learning about other cultures.

Work was another foundation of my upbringing. As early as 8 or 9 years old, I set up lemonade stands, walked dogs, and knocked on neighborhood doors, offering to do projects for a few dollars. In our household, summer jobs were a requirement as soon as we turned 16. But I loved working so much, I started cashiering at our family friend's car wash at age 15 and had part-time jobs all throughout high school and college, as well.

After graduation, while most of my friends took jobs near home, I set off on a totally new adventure—a move to New Jersey to work for AT&T. With my parents pushing me to buy a house as soon as I could, and with real estate prices double what they were in Texas, I partnered with a friend to purchase a home in a desirable neighborhood close to our office. We covered the mortgage by renting rooms to our co-workers. That's when I unexpectedly became a landlord at age 26.

I didn't realize it at the time, but that experience launched my real estate investing journey and, ultimately, a career shift into real estate almost 25 years later. In between, I often dedicated 60+ hours a week to my corporate clients, prioritizing the profits and health of the companies I served over my own.

Throughout my life, those values my parents instilled in me—pursuing new adventures, striving for financial independence, and taking risks—also gave me the courage to quit my corporate job and travel the world for a year, start a successful consulting business and manage multiple side hustles including an e-commerce wine business and writing travel articles.

Today, as a real estate coach and investor, I can work and travel whenever and wherever I want. These influences continue to inspire me to help other women see that they can also live the lives of their dreams.

Think about the personal challenges you've overcome in your life. How did the obstacles that you've overcome play a part in the impact that you make now?

As you can probably guess, it's not easy for me to say no to things. I can't count the number of times when I've taken the whole concept of working hard and devoting myself to other commitments to the extreme. I've always poured myself into whatever I do, and at times, that has come at a cost to my health and happiness.

When I worked in the corporate world, I often put myself and my self-care last, as so many professional women tend to do. I've worked with toxic clients and colleagues and demanding, unappreciative bosses. I used to prioritize work over important events with family and friends, and as a result, I missed the opportunity to create some wonderful memories and experiences.

I don't do that anymore. That's one challenge I have successfully—and happily—overcome.

As an entrepreneur, I get to make my own choices. I decide who I work with, when I work, and where I work. When I do all these things, I'm better able to serve my clients and give them the best version of me.

Looking in from the outside, I see lots of professional women caught up in that same cycle I've been in many times before. By sharing what I've learned and providing an alternative to success beyond the traditional norms, I now strive to support women in creating the lives they deserve.

Reflect on a moment in your professional life that you perceived as a failure. How did this experience lead to your most significant lessons of impact? Share how you have applied these lessons to positively influence your life and the lives of others.

In my late 20s, I quit my job in New York and embarked on a 14-month, around-the-world adventure with one of my best friends. When we returned home, I accepted a role at a marketing agency in San Francisco. My excitement to live in a new city and start a new venture was short-lived, as I realized right away that the work environment and dynamics with my new colleagues were not aligned with my approach and values.

In my heart, I knew I was in the wrong place. But, having just taken a year and a half off work, I told myself that quitting would be failing. The real failure, however, was not being true to myself and watching the job take a toll on my physical and emotional health.

Instead of leaving that job for a better situation, I stayed for four stressful years until the agency let me go during the dotcom bust in the early 2000s. That's when I decided never to allow someone else to control my destiny.

I knew I needed to regroup and reflect before diving into something else. Taking some time off to do what I love most—travel—helped put things in perspective. After a month-long trip to Burma, Thailand, and Cambodia with my sister and my niece, who had just graduated from law school, I turned to entrepreneurship.

With the help of my dear friend Mary, I launched a new career as a corporate communications consultant. And when COVID hit in 2019, I pivoted again—to working full time as a REALTOR and managing my own portfolio of rental properties and Airbnb listings.

Through my own personal journey, I'm now able to educate women on the importance of taking control of their own destinies. My goal is to motivate others to recognize their potential, embrace new opportunities, and make impactful decisions that lead them to a fulfilling and balanced life.

Often the challenges we face lead to the most important lessons, and that's certainly been my experience. I hope I can continue to be a source of inspiration and guidance for others.

How do you ensure your business practices align with ethical and sustainable principles while balancing profitability with making a positive impact?

As an entrepreneur, integrating ethical and sustainable practices into my business is not just a choice, but a responsibility. I've found that treating people with transparency, fairness, and respect naturally creates a positive experience for everyone and ensures profitability and positive impact go hand in hand.

Many of my clients are beginning investors, so education is one of the most important services I provide. Before we even start working together, I give clients information and tips about everything they need to know to make smart, informed decisions. I'm there with them every step of the way, offering guidance, answering questions, and explaining how things work in the process. Even after a deal is closed, I am a resource for follow-up investing questions, and recommending contractors or property management assistance.

Since most of my clients come from within my current network or from referrals, I usually have a good feel for whether we are a good match.

But before we move forward, I set up a call or an in-person meeting to learn more about them, their perspectives, and their goals.

When it comes to profitability, I may have a different view than most entrepreneurs. I've become laser-focused on working only with clients who share my values and approach. Working with people I enjoy and want to spend time is one of my highest priorities. When my energies and ethics aren't aligned with my client's, those relationships no longer serve either person and are not worth the headache or the heartache. In those rare cases, I get to decide to choose happiness over profitability.

I'm committed to maintaining a business model that supports local economies and conservation efforts. Staying informed about the latest trends and best practices also allows me to continuously adapt and improve my strategies.

What role do partnerships and collaborations play in amplifying the impact of your business? How do you identify and cultivate meaningful relationships with other business leaders?

I believe the partnerships and collaborations I've formed throughout my years in business have played a huge role in elevating my offers. I've developed an amazing network of trusted partners that continue to support me and my client base.

I attribute my vast network of friends and colleagues to my multiple passions, love for travel, and genuine curiosity about people. I'm fortunate to have connections not just in the real estate and travel industries, but also across a wide range of professions and interests.

As an extroverted solopreneur, I'm always seeking new friendships and partnerships with like-minded people who have similar goals and who want to make a greater impact in the world. Mastermind and networking groups have provided me with amazing opportunities to meet fellow entrepreneurs across the world. We all get to learn from one another, get good guidance, bounce ideas off each other, and support each other. It's also an avenue for new clients.

When I get into these groups and rooms and start talking with people, learning about their business, and sharing my own business, I can find partnerships and ideas in the most unexpected places.

Over the years, these partnerships have inspired me to pivot from working primarily with people who are buying and selling their homes to focusing on investors. I'm especially interested in helping people buy second homes or vacation rental properties to build wealth while expanding their opportunities for more life experiences and connections.

Travel is such a huge part of my life that I've been thinking about how I can incorporate travel more into what I do. I'm learning that it's not only helping women achieve financial freedom, but also asking what the next step is for them. As I mentioned before, it's about guiding them to create more of these experiences that they love and are super passionate about, spending more time with their loved ones, going on adventures, and seeing the world.

I'm always trying to figure out ways to expand my business to achieve greater results. I think about how I can encourage people to use their financial success to look differently at travel and use their experiences to make an impact in their own lives and communities. Just this year, through some of these connections and partnerships, I'm starting to get ideas and see opportunities to do some unique things in this area.

Looking ahead, what are your aspirations for the future impact of your business and how do you plan to continue evolving and innovating in this area?

I want to continue helping women build their confidence and achieve financial freedom through real estate. I truly believe there's a way I can make an even greater impact by helping shape the experiences and memories they create as a result.

Specifically, I want to extend my mission even further, beyond empowerment, to foster greater communications and interactions between people everywhere. We live in such a crazy world right now, with so much division and chaos. Travel, whether it's across town or across borders, can help reconnect the gaps that have grown in our society.

I'm now partnering with a long-time friend and fellow adventurer to offer women curated experiences to live a life filled with abundance and purpose. I think it's a natural extension to the work I've been doing and the life I've created for myself.

Life is too short to wait for "someday" to experience all the things we're meant to achieve.

So my ultimate goal is to inspire and provide women with opportunities to live life every single day.

That's the impact that I want to make.

you are empowered to choose

CARRIE PERALTA-BRUMMETT

in /carriemperalta

peakstatecoaching.com

Carrie is a 20-year technical recruiter and leader-turned career coach, and diversity, equity, and inclusion (DEI) strategist. Her mission is to empower women and under-represented individuals to thrive in tech careers they love. She is the founder of Peak State Coaching, where she works with clients to help them clarify their future vision, unlock their confidence, shift their mindset, and own their worth. In her free time, she enjoys spending time with her family and friends, practicing yoga, cooking, planning her next travel adventure, and improving Amazon's profits with a large online shopping cart.

How do you define impact?

Impact is something that matters—an effect that is important to you or to someone else, whether it's positive or negative, it leaves an impression.

Looking back over your life, who has impacted you most, and what specific advice or guidance from them has not only influenced your personal growth but also significantly impacted the direction of your professional career?

Family

My father, a dedicated labor union organizer, profoundly impacted my outlook on work and fairness. Witnessing his commitment to organizing for fair wages and better working conditions left an indelible mark on me. Although I chose an adjacent career path in Human Resources (HR) and didn't always share his views on unionization, his belief in the value of dignified employment and fair compensation deeply influenced my professional direction. I embraced his conviction that people deserve fulfilling work, fair pay, and supportive workplaces, shaping my approach to HR and recruiting and my commitment to fostering a positive impact in the workplace.

I also gleaned a lot from my mom, who had a direct communication style. Even as a kid, she asked me, "Do you want to end up pregnant and pumping gas the rest of your life, or make something of yourself?" She was a first-generation Mexican-American and didn't go to college. I look back now and affectionately call this my mom's no-fluff college pep talk. There were no legacy universities or alumni in my family. The legacy was going to start with me.

I hustled my way through college, working two jobs while taking a full course load. To save money, I started at a community college and then transferred to a California State University, majoring in Ethnic Studies. The best part? I graduated without any college debt. I feel especially grateful for this now as I'm acutely aware of the enduring burden that college debt places on people, even well into their careers.

Authors & Influencers

As I was working my way through college, one of the first few self-development/finance books I read was by Suze Orman. I'll never forget her advice, *"Pay yourself first"* advising you to put away money, invest in yourself, even before living expenses, and wherever you put it, don't touch it. I took that as gospel at a young age, set aside a portion of my modest income, saved it, and let it grow through interest.

Another person who had a significant impact on me was Tony Robbins. I was 19, living on my own for the first time, broke, eating ramen or baked potatoes on the cheap, and figuring it out in college while working two jobs.

I vividly remember watching Tony Robbins' cheesy infomercials and being intrigued by his concepts. His advice on mindset resonated with me, and even though I couldn't afford the $250 price tag, I ordered his CDs, taking advantage of the 30-day satisfaction money-back guarantee. I absorbed as much as I could and was inspired by his advice, realizing that his perspective was on a completely different level. I didn't know it at the time, but this experience planted the seed for my future career as a coach. And yes, on the 29th day, I went to a UPS store and shipped all the CDs back for my refund.

Another influencer for me is Brené Brown, an outstanding and talented researcher, psychologist, and thought leader. Her book "Dare to Lead" struck a chord for me when I was in a leadership role without a title. I was intrigued by all of her work on vulnerability and shame. Her book emphasizes leading with a human-first approach, embracing empathy, vulnerability, and self-care. To me, this meant showing up as your authentic self as a leader.

These influences have all helped me, especially during the existential crisis I had when I lost my job at a tech and entertainment giant. I had so much of my identity, earnings, and career tied to my self-worth. When it all disappeared, I had to step back and figure out who I was without this career and what was next for me. I spent a lot of time doing inner work—especially the dark stuff of why my identity was so wrapped up in my career. It was to be my butterfly season where I got curious about myself, my why, and my purpose. It ultimately helped me build resilience versus set me back, and I'm grateful for the experience. It inspired me to move forward and serve others doing what I was most passionate about—empowering underrepresented people to thrive in their tech careers as a coach.

Think about the personal challenges you've overcome in your life. How did the obstacles that you've overcome play a part in the impact that you make now?

Overall, I think of the long game and resilience. What will my decisions today look like in a few weeks, months, or years? What am I doing now that will shape what I want later?

Every day we're empowered with a choice.

I've always been driven by the desire for more—for myself and for my daughter. My sometimes impulsive nature leads me to try new things, but I'm also very conscious of the long game. I think about how today's decisions will shape my future.

Life gets "crunchy." It's not always smooth sailing; there are bumps in the road, curveballs, and distractions that can throw us off course. But I've learned to put on my metaphorical Kevlar vest and *decide* for myself whether to let these challenges penetrate me or bounce off. I choose for them to bounce off and keep pressing on.

When I think about an obstacle versus an opportunity, I can certainly relate to the risk vs reward factor. When I made the decision to join Google, I was recently divorced and a single mom with a preschooler. It meant leaving behind the familiar— leaving a company where I had been successful, and frankly too comfortable, for nearly ten years. I was ready to level up, and that meant pushing myself to step outside my comfort zone. If I hadn't, I would have stayed in career stagnation.

This move was particularly challenging as it required me to relocate to the pricey Silicon Valley and away from family and friends. I was both scared and exhilarated by the opportunity. The decision to pursue this career opportunity wasn't without its critics. It meant that I was leaving my mom, which isn't widely accepted in Hispanic culture. Some in my family thought I was crazy and gave me the "you're choosing your career over family" guilt trip. But I knew that this opportunity was worth it. It would open up so many more opportunities to stretch my thinking, expand my skills, develop my circle of influence, and I would have a direct impact on bringing in talent for an amazing company and culture.

I CAN CHOOSE WHAT COMES NEXT.

When it comes to feeling the fear and doing it anyway, I've delved deep into the emotional aspects of this. Being curious about myself has been crucial for my journey. I've learned to take a moment to understand why I feel a certain way, why

I'm frustrated, scared, or experiencing self-doubt—
imposter syndrome is real.

I've realized that it's not about having all the
answers, but about pausing and being aware of my
emotions, asking myself why I might be feeling this
way, or where it's coming from. Then comes the
magical part:

I can choose what comes next.

I can let unhelpful thoughts spiral downward, or
acknowledge them and refocus my mindset on what
I do want to focus on. This self-awareness has been
invaluable in helping me pick myself up and keep
moving forward, always keeping my eyes on the long-
term vision I have for my life.

———————

*Reflect on a moment in your professional life that
you perceived as a failure. How did this experience
lead to your most significant lessons of impact?
Share how you have applied these lessons to
positively influence your life and the lives of others.*

When I unexpectedly lost my corporate job in
2023, I spent a lot of time reflecting and learning

about myself, trying to find the nuggets in my circumstances. I initially felt like I had failed and disappointed myself and was faced with unpacking my identity and who I was without this career that I wrapped myself around for so long.

This time I wanted to lean in and think about what happened, process it, and sit with it. In the past, I would avoid introspection and throw myself into my work and not deal with all the crunchy bits like feeling sad or mad, telling myself I didn't have time for that. I wanted to get stuff done, check things off my list, and move on, but that was just denial.

Instead, I chose to see it as an opportunity, even though it felt like a setback. I took the time to consider what was important to me and what I wanted for my future. During this time, I (finally) invested in myself with Tony Robbins coaching, completing all of the Mastery courses and working with a coach. It was hands down the best money I've ever spent and changed my life profoundly. I had such clarity about who I was and what was next for me.

In a million years, I never thought I would be an entrepreneur. It's hard work, and I have to put in long hours, figure out a lot of things that I know nothing

about with limited resources, and be a bootstrapped, one-woman show. I only knew corporate life, but I didn't like corporate politics or bureaucracy. I have a very egalitarian approach. We all put our pants on the same way, one leg at a time. I care about meaningful work, helping people, and getting things done.
Then I thought about what I truly love to do, which is recruiting people and helping them achieve their dream careers. I just loved it and found it immensely rewarding.

I have had the privilege of meeting many talented people throughout my career. It has been an honor for me to help these individuals achieve their dream careers, improve their lives with competitive pay, and work on really cool projects while impacting their families and career trajectories. Reflecting on this, I started thinking about coaching others and using the skills I have acquired to guide people in discovering their aspirations and what truly brings them joy. I connected the dots and realized that I could do this in my own unique way, by meeting individuals where they are and showing them the possibilities available to them. The cool part is that it's already within them.

I'm just pulling the curtain back a bit.

How do you ensure your business practices align with ethical and sustainable principles while balancing profitability with making a positive impact?

As I embarked on this venture, I took it very seriously. Money was not my primary motivation. My main goal was to help others be the best version of themselves and align that with their careers. When I work with my clients, I give them my full attention because I understand they are investing in themselves as well as in me. I want to ensure they get the most out of our time together.

When it comes to ethics, I strive to do the right thing because I believe it has a ripple effect and can have a positive impact. Empowering women can lead to the empowerment of other women. I don't see it as a competition. There is enough success for everyone.

The approach to coaching work depends on the individual I'm working with, as everyone is at a different stage in their career and has different needs. I listen, am honest, provide sound guidance, and base my advice on credible data and insights so that it is bespoke to each individual.

When considering sustainability, I have been determined to expand my coaching business so that my methods and strategies can be taught to more coaches as we grow the team and further develop to reach even more people. Eventually, I hope to transition out of the business, retire, and enjoy my best life while the business continues to thrive and serve. I envision it being able to sustain itself beyond my lifetime and continue to evolve in the future.

———

Looking ahead, what are your aspirations for the future impact of your business, and how do you plan to continue evolving and innovating in this area?

Scale and impact are my focus for this year. I plan to expand my business's reach, making a greater impact in serving others.

I've just launched High Impact Days. The first offering is a High Impact Day focused on Mastering Interviews. During this day, I will work with clients one-on-one to address their biggest interview challenges and help them confidently and authentically communicate their career accomplishments and how they add value to the company's objectives.

I am developing a group coaching program where we will delve deeper into my proven methods, which include career strategy, gaining clarity, taking action for progress, and fostering a sense of community within the cohort. Building community is vital, especially for those navigating job transitions or experiencing burnout. It's easy for people to isolate themselves and feel overwhelmed. By being part of a cohort, they can find the support and encouragement they need.

This community will be made up of individuals who are rooting for each other to succeed, creating a powerful network of mutual support and accountability.

I'm very passionate about achieving fair and competitive pay for women and women of color. Many women struggle with discussing and negotiating their compensation, whether it's asking for a salary increase or negotiating during job offers. I want to empower them to advocate for themselves. It's important to ask for the pay you deserve and not settle. You've worked hard to get where you are, and you should feel good about your compensation. This is a topic I'm working on for another High Impact Day, focusing on having Confident Pay Conversations.

Looking ahead, I plan to develop online coaching courses to make them flexible and accessible to people when they need it.

I'm here to serve those ready for more in their lives and careers.

from heartache to healing

A MOM'S MISSION TO RETHINK FOOD AND CHANGE HEALTH TRAJECTORIES

TISHA CASTILLO

in /tishacastillo

tishacastillo.com

Tisha (with no "R") is a special needs mom, wife, and a Metabolic Health Nutritionist who rises before the sun, champions the underdog, dances like no one's watching, and debunks aging and genetic myths in health and nutrition. Her love for the outdoors, her fur babies, and her kids, and her fight against misleading health narratives fuel her mission to change health trajectories and heal the world.

With a background in both conventional and holistic health, Tisha's journey began with personal challenges that reshaped her understanding of true health. Diagnosed with PCOS and initially told she could never have children, she defied the odds and now proudly raises two wonderful kids. Her daughter's special needs and her son's heart condition further ignited her passion for uncovering the root causes of chronic health issues.

A metabolic health practitioner, functional diagnostic nutritionist, and board-certified health and wellness coach, Tisha combines her extensive training with her real-life experiences to offer practical, sustainable health solutions. She believes in the power of generational health, helping parents improve their well-being to ensure a healthier future for their children and grandchildren.

Through her virtual health practice, Simplified Health & Nutrition, Tisha rethinks our approach to food and cuts through the nutrition noise. She's here to help guide people to live a life where aging without chronic health conditions is their reality, not a lifetime dependency on medications or supplements—a life where achievers like you and I can thrive, not just survive. Tisha's approach is simple yet powerful, aiming to empower individuals to take control of their health with confidence and clarity. Join her mission to rethink food and change your health trajectory.

How do you define impact?

Over the years, my definition of impact has evolved. Today, I see impact as leaving the world a better place than I found it. It's about empowering people to make their own positive changes.

In my work, my main focus is generational health. Being part of the sandwich generation, I have many friends who care for elderly parents and their own children, all while battling chronic health conditions. When surrounded by sickness and pain, it's overwhelming and scary. It has become something people accept "as is," as if there is no control over health as you age.

The day it hit me that my daughter might outlive me was life-changing.

I knew I had to be healthy enough to care for her for as long as possible. I couldn't and wouldn't rely on her to care for me or put that burden on my son. I wanted to break the cycle and give them every chance to live long and fulfilling lives, without chronic conditions. And I wanted to be an active part of it.

When I ask my clients how important it is to give their kids every advantage while reducing their risk for chronic health conditions, they are all in. When I ask who will take care of them and if they want to burden their children or spouse, something shifts inside them. That, to me, is IMPACT, and why generational health is the foundation of my desire to heal the world.

Looking back over your life, who has impacted you most, and what specific advice or guidance from them has not only influenced your personal growth but also significantly impacted the direction of your professional career?

My daughter has impacted my life the most. As a kid, I wanted to be a doctor and a mom because I was going to heal the world. As a teenager, I was told I'd never be able to have children. My doctor told me, "It doesn't appear you have a uterus, so childbearing just can't happen." Bomb dropped. Accept it and move on. (I later found out I had PCOS. My missing uterus was the result of a cyst that had grown so large it covered my uterus, making it undetectable on an ultrasound.)

While I'd like to say that this experience made me want to find a solution, it didn't. I was a rule follower and took the diagnosis as a permanent condition that I had no control over.

I was always interested in the human body and have studied it since I was a little girl. One of my first requested gifts was a set of human body encyclopedias as an elementary school child because I wanted to learn everything about the body. As I got older, knowing that I'd never be able to give birth, took a toll on me. I continued following the rules for health but continued to be diagnosed with different conditions. I even had a cancer scare. None of it made sense, but that's just how it was.

It wasn't until I took control of my body and found out what was going on with it that I was able to have two kids, first my daughter, and then my son.

My daughter is my "why." She was that miracle baby I never thought I'd have. She let me be the one thing I always wanted to be: a mom. It wasn't easy. I had a very difficult pregnancy. She was born 7 weeks early and was immediately put into the NICU. The docs said she wouldn't make it past three days, then three months, then three years. Now, she's in her thirties, so once again, docs don't know it all. Once I became a mom, everything I thought I was supposed to be doing for everybody else no longer mattered. It was about how I could refocus on this amazing being that I was now fortunate enough to be responsible for.

IT WAS AT THAT MOMENT THAT I KNEW I HAD TO TAKE CONTROL OF HER LIFE, HER HEALTH, AND BE HER MOM.

She had special needs and was medically fragile. I was told after she was born that "G-d gives children with special needs to parents with special abilities," and that stuck with me. I felt so blessed to have her in my life. I accepted all the treatments, meds, and procedures the docs prescribed because I believed they knew it all. They wanted so desperately to label her condition, and the first 18 months of her life were filled with doctor appointments, medication trials, travel to specialists, therapies, all of it. I eventually said, "I don't care what you call it anymore. Just teach me how to live with this. If I can make changes, great. But if not, if her life is almost over at 18 months old, I'm done with looking for a diagnosis to try more medications. I just want to know how to give her the best life she can have for the time she has left." Her pediatrician looked at me and told me he had no idea.

It was at that moment that I knew I had to take control of her life, her health, and be her mom.

I didn't stop going to follow-up appointments or take her off meds, but I was done trying to figure out what to call it. I learned to help keep her alive and taught her how to live. She learned how to laugh, have fun, sit still, be patient, and engage. She helped me prepare for my son.

My son was born several years later (getting pregnant isn't easy with PCOS). While my pregnancy was much easier, the delivery was not. His cord was wrapped around his neck, and I had to have an emergency C-section. They needed to save him, and they did. When I was finally able to hold him, I knew something wasn't right. He wasn't breathing right. He didn't look right. He was stressed. He was struggling. He was so tired. When I brought my concerns to the hospital doctor, he told me, "You're just a young worried mom. You both had a traumatic delivery. He'll be fine." I bit my tongue and felt heartbroken. Was I wrong? Was I making a big deal out of nothing? Was I not going to be a good mom to a non-special needs child?

After being released from the hospital, I followed up with my daughter's pediatrician. He listened to me. He immediately responded, and guess what? We found out my son was born with 2 holes in his heart and was literally drowning. After a couple of weeks of trying to manage his symptoms with meds, which didn't work, he had open-heart surgery at six weeks old. If I had accepted what the docs had said and didn't trust my gut, my knowledge, and my life experiences with my daughter, I would have missed the symptoms, and my son might not be here today.

My daughter helped keep him alive by teaching me what I needed to know to be a good mom to him, too. When I think of both of my children, they're my "why," and the impact they have had on me is real. I was able to step outside what was expected of me and be the mom I always wished I had.

I also learned that medicine doesn't fix it all.

People who practice conventional medicine don't know it all; they only know what they're taught, which in the nutrition space is about 12 hours total if they're lucky. I know what I've learned over the last 30-plus years of being a mom and doing my own research. That experience and knowledge fuel my work every day, helping people determine the root cause of their conditions. I help them change their health trajectory so they're not burdened with pain and disease, and they stop getting sicker, younger, and dying sooner than they're supposed to. Even better, I do it in a way that is Simple AF.

———

Think about the personal challenges you've overcome in your life. How did the obstacles that you've overcome play a part in the impact that you make now?

Growing up, I was that rule-following, people-pleasing, perfection-seeking kind of girl. My world was dictated by what everybody else wanted me to be. I thought I was exceptional at being a chameleon because I could fit any role you wanted me to have. I followed the rules.

After becoming a mom and following all the rules in health, medicine, and life, things weren't going the way they were supposed to. I kept thinking I wasn't doing enough and had to keep pushing and doing more.

Over the last 15 years, I've realized there's a reason why rules are repeated—it's easier to go along with life than to challenge what you're supposed to be doing. If I had gone along with what I was told, I probably would've never gotten married. After having my daughter, I would have listened to the doctors who told me they didn't know how to "live with this" and would've put her into a home when she was a year old. That's what I was told to do since it would ruin my life to continue to take care of her.

Looking back, it's ironic that I always wanted to be in healthcare, thinking it meant practicing conventional medicine. Now, I see that one of my biggest hurdles is battling those traditional practices.

I can't follow the rules because the rules don't work.

I went back to school to get my degree to learn the latest and greatest, and they taught me all the things I know I'd never tell someone to do because it doesn't help you get better. It just makes you dependent on medication as you continue to get sicker. Managing symptoms that are going to get progressively worse is what conventional medicine teaches us— medicate, and when that stops working, operate. Breaking through that and being okay with beating to a different drum, walking a different path, and impacting the lives of those around me is a struggle. It inspires and scares me a little bit because I still fall back into that rule-following person sometimes. But I had to break the rules. Go against the grain. If I hadn't, my children wouldn't be here. I don't know where I would have ended up or how sick I would be today, and I definitely wouldn't be on a mission to heal the world.

Stepping out and sharing what I know has been the biggest challenge but helps reinforce that I'm on the right path.

Reflect on a moment in your professional life that you perceived as a failure. How did this experience lead to your most significant lessons of impact? Share how you have applied these lessons to positively influence your life and the lives of others.

I wouldn't call it a professional failure, but a disappointment. In my late thirties, I decided to follow my passion and learn more about health and the human body. My daughter was battling numerous medical issues that she wasn't supposed to have because I followed all the rules. As I started implementing what I knew to work, people noticed and asked me questions because they saw things improve for both me and my daughter.

As a rule follower, it was very difficult. I said, "I can't tell you those things. I don't have credentials. I'm not licensed. I don't have a degree. I'm going to get in trouble." So, I went back to school to get my degree, believing that credentials would improve my reach, capacity, and ability to communicate with people. Within a couple of months, I realized I couldn't quit, but everything I was learning was exactly why we're all getting sicker.

It was a gut punch. I was trying to figure out how I could have the most impact, be the most credible, and have all the information. Going back to school at an older age is challenging and expensive—financially, emotionally, physically, and mentally. Despite the challenges, I didn't quit. I graduated, spoke at my graduation, and was awarded Outstanding Student in Dietetics & Nutrition by the state chapter of AND. I became a board-certified health and wellness coach, earned my credentials as a functional diagnostic nutritionist, and later credentialed as a metabolic health practitioner, allowing me to focus on metabolic health as my specialty.

I have all the degrees and credentials one would need to look good on paper, but it's my understanding and experience that has allowed me to create solutions that work. I take what big food and big pharma want me to know and challenge it with what I know works. This journey has taught me to trust myself and be okay with the fact that I am on the right path. Different avenues of learning opened up a global educational system for me to learn more and become the specialist I am today.

So while it's not necessarily a failure, I was hoping it would have given me what I needed. What I've learned, however, is that I need to trust myself and be confident enough to share that, because what I know works.

How do you ensure your business practices align with ethical and sustainable principles while balancing profitability with making a positive impact?

My business focus is sustainability for my clients. I can't just teach you something to improve your health in 30 days and be done with it. I need to help you integrate what you learn into your life so you can sustain it long-term. If you don't understand it, you can't teach your kids, siblings, or parents. My goal of generational health fails if I can't help you sustain it.

Ethically, I'm a recovering enabler, now working to empower others. I want people to make decisions that work for them and guide them to ensure they're on the right path. If I can make an impact and help someone live a healthier life, profitability will follow. I'm not selling products for the sake of it.

There's little money in health, but a lot in sickness—that's why our healthcare system is really a sickness industry.

I know how to work with different personalities. I pride myself on asking questions and helping people figure out how to integrate what they want into their world. If I can help you focus on your health today so you don't have to focus on illness tomorrow, profitability will follow naturally, both for my passion and for my pocketbook. While profitability is important, I'm more interested in the passion of ensuring people heal.

Looking ahead, what are your aspirations for the future impact of your business, and how do you plan to continue evolving and innovating in this area?

I'm a lifelong learner. I spend so much time learning, analyzing, and researching. Unfortunately, nutritional science isn't science anymore. It's been muddied by monetary influences, dictating what gets published and what stories get picked up—whether you should have a glass of wine or three Oreos before bed to be healthy.

I've realized that while I want to help people with very specific conditions, what excites me most is the ability to share more foundational information with a larger audience. Many people don't realize they're dealing with metabolic dysfunction—it's not a common term and isn't often diagnosed. It isn't something you can manage with a pill.

I want to share more about what metabolic dysfunction is, why it's important, and what symptoms and conditions are tied to it. Whether you're six or sixty, there are basic things you can do to get on the right path. If you need to dive deeper after those initial steps, I can help with that too.

I'm excited about sharing foundational knowledge that can impact more people and increase problem awareness. As long as you're willing to ask questions and learn, I'm willing to teach. That's what I hope to achieve moving forward.

the impact of storytelling

SARA DAVENPORT

in /sara-davenport-journalist

saradavenport.net

Sara is an award-winning TV anchor who spent decades on-air with NBC. While anchoring the morning news in front of 4 million people in Houston, Sara decided she was tired of covering breaking news and chasing hurricanes; she wanted to chase her kids instead! Sara made the rare move of walking away from a TV career in her prime to pursue her passions and spend time with her husband and four boys.

Sara got clear on her passions and purpose: sharing other's stories, helping women to create multiple streams of income, and helping others to create a LIFE and not just living. This multi-passionate entrepreneur has done so by becoming a true-crime investigative journalist and on-camera coach for Fortune 500 companies, and she joined the social selling company (Arbonne) and was promoted to the top 1% of the company in under 2 years.

Sara also coaches other TV anchors and reporters to help them find their passions outside of the toxic news industry and reminds them (and everyone) that you don't have to be a "one-trick pony!" Most recently, she launched the Storyteller's Experience, where she helps entrepreneurs share their stories in a way that converts to impact and income. After all, if you lean into the power of the pivot, you might just design a life you love!

How do you define impact?

Interestingly, the word impact has been a central part of my life for well over a decade. When there is impact, you are making an impression on someone or on something that causes it or them to change. I love the word impact because I believe impact can lead to legacy. If you want to give more, do more, have more, be more, share more, and bless more, it all comes back to impacting others. And when you impact others, you create a legacy.

Legacy isn't something a lot of people think about, but here's the truth:

You're creating a legacy every year with your actions, your career, your decisions, and the precious time you spend with your family.

Looking back over your life, who has impacted you most, and what specific advice or guidance from them has not only influenced your personal growth but also significantly impacted the direction of your professional career?

I can't narrow it down to just one person who's impacted me the most. There are so many. I decided to focus on two very powerful women.

My mom is one of the most powerful, influential, and impactful women I know. Her name is Diane Allen. She was one of the first female TV anchors to be on the air, starting in the early 1970s. My mom won multiple Emmys. She traveled around the world as a broadcaster in different war-torn areas. She sat in the Oval Office, interviewing different presidents and sharing stories from all over the world. What I love about my mom is that she left people better than she found them.

When she interviewed them and shared their stories, she had an impact on them. So many people wanted to be around her. They wanted to be like her, and they still do. I was one of them. I wanted to be just like her.

In fact, she inspired me to go into journalism. From the time I was five, I would go around telling people I would be a TV anchor and reporter: I wanted to be a storyteller. I got my first on-air job right out of college, working in a tiny town in Upstate NY. Getting to tell people's stories, and make an impact on the community, is what got me out of bed on Monday mornings. I loved every bit of it! I got to share stories and make an impact the way my mom did. My mom continued her legacy of impact by serving as a State Senator for over 2 decades in the Northeast. There's legislation named after her, the Diane Allen Equal Pay Act, in the state of New Jersey. She's had a massive impact on me and others. She created an impact on my life by showing me I can do whatever I set my mind out to do. She gave me the courage to go after my dreams. And she reminded me that we need to pull others up with us, along our way. It's not just what we can do to help ourselves and our families, but it's so important to have a positive impact on others as we move through life. I am so proud to be her daughter!

The other woman who's impacted me most is Rita Davenport. My married name is Davenport, so people would think I was her daughter, but I'm not. But like my mom, Rita has had a ripple effect of impact in my life.

Rita was the president of the social selling company I joined shortly after leaving the television news industry. That woman has had a lasting impact on me. She taught me to believe in people big enough to the point where they start to believe in themselves. So many people lack belief in their dreams, abilities, and the beauty of their stories.

Rita taught me about the importance of personal development. I joke that my car is like a rolling university. I always have podcasts on, or I'm listening to different audible books.

She showed me the importance of investing in yourself because the mind is so powerful, and she taught me that what you think about is what you bring about. You've got to mind your mind. Rita used to say, "Do a checkup from the neck up, because energy follows thoughts. If you want it bad enough, whatever it is, and if you're willing to persist until it happens, the world will step aside for the person who knows where they're going." I would take all these great "Rita-isms" into my life along with all the knowledge, belief, and power that my mom poured into me.

I have achieved what I have set my mind to. I wanted to be a Division One tennis player. I did that. I wanted to go into TV, and I made it to a top station. I wanted to inspire others to speak on big stages, and I've done that. It's because of these two women who poured into me: my mom, from the time I was a baby, and

Rita, from the time I was in my early thirties. They poured into me so that my life was more than I could ever imagine. And now I'm so excited to be a multi-passionate entrepreneur.

I followed my dreams, and my life is full of *"get-to's"* instead of *"have-to's."* They taught me how to dream. My goal is to pour what I've learned into those who come behind me, to teach them how to live their life using their God-given talents and passions, so they too can live a life they design, not just a life by default.

Think about the personal challenges you've overcome in your life. How did the obstacles that you've overcome play a part in the impact that you make now?

From an outside perspective, it might seem like I've had this perfect life, and everything always went exactly according to plan, but that's not true. Nobody gets out of this life without going through many bumps and valleys and leaving with many bruises.

God never promises us an easy path through life. One thing that my mentor Rita Davenport said was, "Prepare for impact because it's coming. If you prepare, you can handle that impact, good or bad, but you need to prepare." When my husband was diagnosed with cancer, I wasn't prepared for those words, but it impacted us. My husband was diagnosed with colon cancer about 10 years ago. I have four boys, ranging from newborn to 12 at the time. That was difficult, but I learned the impact that my faith would have on me so that I could turn to God.

IF YOU BUILD YOUR DREAMS AND BANK ACCOUNT, YOU'LL BE PREPARED FOR IMPACT.

I could trust His plan in that diagnosis. I learned the impact of having the right circle of friends of support around you. I learned the impact of having multiple streams of income. When Rita would say prepare for impact, she also always said, "Build it before you need it, because you never know what's coming."

If you build your dreams and bank account, you'll be prepared for impact.

You might not be prepared on that day per se, but when the dust settles, you are prepared. I am so thankful that I had prepared for all of that.

Reflect on a moment in your professional life that you perceived as a failure. How did this experience lead to your most significant lessons of impact? Share how you have applied these lessons to positively influence your life and the lives of others.

Some people dwell on failures in their professional life. I've taken so many great lessons out of it because we all fail. There were times when I failed daily. Being on television, the word "no" could not affect you.

If my producer told me I had to go out and get a story because a child was tragically killed, I had to go get the interview, find out who the child was, and interview the parents. It's incredibly hard knocking on the door of a parent whose child has just passed away. But I couldn't come back without a story because there can't even be a 1-minute hole in the newscast—you can't have blank air.

I had to find my way around the word "no" a lot. That was hard. There were a lot of low moments in the TV industry, and what most people don't understand is that the world of television news is a very toxic world, especially today.

The news we cover is very rarely positive, and the environment in which I worked was also very toxic.

From the outside, everything looked perfect. I had a big house, nice cars, a swimming pool, and a boat. I had a smile on my face, and my family was dressed to match in all our Christmas cards.

Behind closed doors, it was a totally different story. I was miserable and put on a facade when things were falling apart. I told people I was fine, while there were nights that I would be in tears in my closet as I pulled out my outfit to wear the next morning.

I'd be in tears asking, "Lord, why am I here? I made it. I did it. I checked all the boxes and hit all the goals. I'm in my dream city."

"There are 4 million people watching me every morning, and yet... I'm miserable."

I wanted to be a present parent. I wanted to chase my kids and not chase breaking news. I wanted to surround myself with people who built others up, not people who tear others down. I was tired of constantly being in the public eye, under scrutiny.

I was tired of being tired.

I knew I should be grateful. After all, more than 16,000 people graduate a year wanting to become on-camera journalists. Why was I miserable? I made it and was working in a top TV station in the nation. Why did God allow me to go through that? I believe that happened so I could step into the next chapter of my life. Had those things not happened, I never would've closed the door on my professional journey in TV. I wouldn't have looked into entrepreneurship.

I come from a long line of inventors and entrepreneurs. But at that time, I couldn't see it. I couldn't see the forest through the trees. I couldn't see the big picture. I was at such a low point in my personal and professional life. If I was going to get out of this funk and toxic career, it was up to me. I decided to bless and release those people in my life and that career, turn the page, and start writing a new chapter. And the new chapter would be a life chasing the unfulfilled dreams that were still in my heart.

I listened to podcasts, read books, and invested in myself. I sought out optimistic people who did things that I wanted to do, and I decided to change the trajectory of my career and the impact I could have *by living a life that I designed.*

How do you ensure your business practices align with ethical and sustainable principles while balancing profitability with making a positive impact?

I'm big on surrounding myself with people who make me better. You must be careful who you surround yourself with.

You are the average of the 5 people you spend the most time with. Think about this: Who are the people you allow to influence you and speak into your life? Be careful of the complainers and the pessimists. They might be dragging you down without you even realizing it. And because I believe that the impact you can make is often times based on who surrounds you, so I surround myself with people I value—people I look up to, respect, enjoy, and who bring me joy.

I surround myself with people who are like my "virtual" board of directors. People who can hold me accountable, push me when needed, and earnestly want my business to be not only sustainable and profitable but also impactful. When it comes to business, I listen to people who've done what I want to do and have gone before me. Never let negative thoughts and words from people tear you down— especially when it comes from someone who hasn't been where you want to go! Take counsel and advice from people who have been successful in business. My ethics, character, and business principles line up with those I look up to. Those are some of the key features of the women who I've chosen to be on my "virtual" board of directors. They're my biggest cheerleaders, and I'm so thankful for them!

———————————

Looking ahead, what are your aspirations for the future impact of your business, and how do you plan to continue evolving and innovating in this area?

I am a multi-passionate entrepreneur. I constantly try to find ways to use the skills, talents, and passions that God has instilled in me to make a future impact on more people. Without a doubt, storytelling is at the heart of all of my entrepreneurial endeavors. I've known the power of telling an impactful story for decades—since my first job with NBC when I was 22 years old.

Today, I serve entrepreneurs by giving them the tools they need to tell their own stories. I founded a LinkedIn Marketing Agency, called "The Hook and the Heart." Because when you have a good hook to your story, and you connect with someone's heart, magic happens! Then combine the right storytelling techniques with the power of LinkedIn—and watch out, world! Big things are coming!

For entrepreneurs who want to learn the art of storytelling themselves, I recently kicked off "The Storytellers Experience." It's like a peek behind the curtain of how journalists do what they do. I teach them how to write content that converts, how to share their stories in impactful ways, and how to get the media coverage they want. I love teaching someone how to write their own press release and get featured on TV. Seeing the impact my storytelling techniques and insider knowledge has on entrepreneurs, as it elevates their own brands, brings me such joy!

As for my long-term plans? I plan to continue to design a life I love and inspire others to live up to their God-given potential along the way.

rejection is redirection

JAMIE MCKINNEY

in /jamie-dandar-mckinney

jamiemckinney.com

Jamie Dandar McKinney, MBA, is an award-winning coach and the best-selling author of *Speak Up, Sister!* Recognized as an Emerging Training Leader and a Top Woman in Energy, Jamie jokes that her stilettos have steel toes. After 2 decades in male-dominated industries, Jamie mastered building confidence as deliberately as building muscle and leading with authenticity.

Through her dynamic programs—The 3 Pillars of Leadership and Speak UP to Level UP®—she empowers you to ditch doubts, amplify your voice, and propel your career. Get ready for results with Coach Jamie rooting for you!

How do you define impact?

Impact is inspired action. It's as simple as that.

A pure definition of impact implies motion. One thing bumps into another, causing a chain reaction. Whether it's a pebble or a boulder, when you throw it in water, it makes a ripple. That's how I think of impact.

Looking back over your life, who has impacted you most, and what specific advice or guidance from them has not only influenced your personal growth but also significantly impacted the direction of your professional career?

I would love to share 2 names in particular because they both prompted pivotal points in my career. The first one is a gentleman named Rich.

When I started my career, I was in the automotive refinishing industry. I was the third female to join a team of 400. On average, I was 20 years younger than everyone else, and I hadn't grown up in the industry.

If we were playing a game of "which one of these things is not like the others," that was me on many levels. I was at my very first sales conference, at 23 years old, and I had never experienced anything like this. It was a bunch of men at a conference center in Scottsdale, Arizona.

Rich was the highest-level person there. It was a big deal that he was there because he didn't always come to these events, and when he walked through the room, people would whisper his name as if he were untouchable.

And I thought: "Now *that's the guy that I have to meet.*"

> *I've always challenged myself to pick out the most intimidating person in a room and introduce myself to them.*

I waited for the right moment, then went up to Rich. I extended my hand and introduced myself. He looked at me and my credential badge, and he said, "Tell me about yourself, Jamie. What have you been up to? Where did you come from?"

We started a conversation, and fast-forward—that conversation turned into a follow-up email, which then turned into a flight reservation, which then had me going to headquarters to meet the highest-level female in the $8 billion company that I worked for.

To this day, I remember some of the advice and guidance that she gave me. She instantly took me under her wing as a mentor, all because I had that conversation with Rich. I think about how different my life would be had we not met. That one conversation changed the trajectory of my career in the automotive industry.

Later on in my career, I changed industries and a few other things were bubbling up. The short version of the story is that I got let go from the company I was working for under some really poor and questionable circumstances. I felt stabbed in the back.

At that time, the career I have now was already in the works, even though I didn't fully realize it at the time. I had a book of my own in the works, *Speak up, Sister!*, and I hired a business coach. He was the first person to say to me, "Jamie, did you know that you were born to be a coach?"

I said, "No, Travis, tell me more. What are the indicators? What does that mean?" As he shared, he added, "This is your calling. This is your purpose, and I'm going to help you with this," and he did.

As he helped me, I organically received requests for coaching services. I built a program, and today, that program has received accolades. I consider it such an honor and a privilege to be able to do for others today, what Travis did for me then.

———————

Think about the personal challenges you've overcome in your life. How did the obstacles that you've overcome play a part in the impact that you make now?

There are so many words that you can associate with challenges. They can be obstacles, opportunities, failures, mistakes, or successes. The outcome of a challenge is greatly impacted by how you're framing it.

WITH CHALLENGES, I'VE LEARNED TO FRAME THEM AS PUZZLES RATHER THAN PROBLEMS.

In my life, there have been challenges, disappointments, and things that sting at the moment. There have been times when I've waited for a silver lining to come, and it has, and there have been other times when I've waited for a silver lining to come, and it didn't. I had to be very intentional about finding one because I was at a place where I just didn't want to accept that the story ended where it did—for instance, when I got let go from a job or had some losses in my personal life. I refused to accept that the book ended there, and I also realized that nobody else was going to continue to write it for me.

With challenges, I've learned to frame them as puzzles rather than problems.

I think of a puzzle as something that's fun. We worked on them as kids. We all worked on them during the pandemic. A puzzle is something that, when you're in it, can be complex. But simultaneously, are you forgiving of yourself when you take a piece and don't immediately put it where it belongs? Sometimes, you have to turn it in different ways or put it in a different spot. When you keep that mindset, one of curiosity and exploration, it might get frustrating here and there, but you continue to move forward. How rewarding is it when you find the spot where that piece fits?

It's all about perspective. If you think about something as a problem, it's problematic, and that instantly starts to garner feelings of negativity, a lack of creativity, or focusing too much on the "how" but not the "what."

Solving a problem is very difficult, whereas exploring a *puzzle* is a much more action-driven, forgiving, exciting, approach.

———————

Reflect on a moment in your professional life that you perceived as a failure. How did this experience lead to your most significant lessons of impact? Share how you have applied these lessons to positively influence your life and the lives of others.

When I had what I call my dramatic departure from the corporate world, I was working on an exclusively male-dominated team. I was the only female on the team.

It had been a particularly challenging season for me personally. I lost a couple of friends tragically. I silently suffered through a miscarriage because there was no one at work who I would ever think about entrusting with that information. Then, I got let go by a narcissist who lied about my performance to protect his.

I vividly remember that it was a Tuesday, and my in-laws were in town. They live many states away. They're rarely in town, and I just couldn't help but think, *Oh gosh, do I feel like the daughter-in-law of the year driving home at 11:30 AM on a Tuesday.*

Months earlier, though, I had started dabbling with writing my book. I shared the idea with a friend, and unbeknownst to me, he had shared my idea with a friend who owns a publishing company. That publisher, out of the blue, called me one day, months before I was let go from my job.

At first, I thought someone was playing a joke on me because, in the publishing world, it's not typical for a publisher to reach out like that.

Because I still had my full-time job, I asked her if I could hold on to her number. Should my priority shift, I asked if I could call her. She said, "Sure." So, on that Tuesday morning, when I got let go, I texted her on my way home and asked if she could meet for coffee the next day.

She responded right away and agreed to meet. After that conversation, combined with a need for over-due self-care, and support from my husband, I took the rest of the year off and made writing my book my job.

I scheduled four-hour blocks to write. There were times that I sat down, and while still grieving the loss of my friends and my miscarriage, I sat down at my desk while wiping away tears. However, writing the book and pouring into my future readers was healing for me. *This* was now my job. I found purpose in it despite being let go from my corporate job.

How do you ensure your business practices align with ethical and sustainable principles while balancing profitability with making a positive impact?

Gut feelings are a huge indicator. Create enough space and allow yourself the opportunity to *feel* a decision rather than just make a decision. One of the things I particularly love about what I do now is that I lead with my ethics and undoubtedly follow a moral compass that points north.

There's a saying that "the softest pillow is a clear conscience." I value my sleep, and I don't want anything interfering with the softness of my pillow, certainly not my conscience.

Starting a business has its challenges. I started my business in 2020, at the height of the pandemic. My revenue that year was almost identical to my salary from my first job out of college, which was over 20 years earlier. However, it was much different from my big-girl corporate salary.

It took discipline to stay committed to revenue-generating activity and put volunteering on the side. I wanted to offer things for free and do volunteer work, but that didn't pay the mortgage. But you know what? My mindset shifted, and I thought—

"The more I build my business, the more generous I can be."

Fast-forward to last year, I was excited to offer scholarships to an online course that I have called Speak UP to Level UP®. Moving forward, I'm focusing on how I can create space now that I have a profitable business that is driving impact and success while giving back more of my physical time as well.

You have to think long-term and be disciplined, prioritizing your business's needs over what your ego may suggest you do.

What role do partnerships and collaborations play in amplifying the impact of your business? How do you identify and cultivate meaningful relationships with other business leaders?

Closing my first five-figure deal was hugely exciting to me. When it happened I was sitting in my office by myself. I high-fived the air and then myself... on the forehead. I realized how ridiculous I looked smacking my own head, even though, there was no one to see!

I'm an extrovert. I enjoy having a group of people, so being a solopreneur during a pandemic was a huge change.

If I were to offer advice on this, I would suggest joining something bigger than you, where the people in the room are smarter than you. The right business mastermind, for example, can be a great fit

I'm currently enrolled in my third or fourth mastermind. I don't have all the answers, and I enjoy collaborating with others in masterminds to generate new ideas.

That's where that abundance piece comes into play. Intentionally putting yourself in groups that are aligned with your values helps to fill the gaps. It strengthens ideas and drives innovation... and helps maintain sanity in the meantime!

———————

Looking ahead, what are your aspirations for the future impact of your business and how do you plan to continue evolving and innovating in this area?

I get so excited about this. I had a baby in March. I'm thrilled to share that while on maternity leave, thirteen women who graduated from my 3 Pillars of Leadership course earned promotions. 13. That was a record-setting number of promotions in that amount of time.

Dollar-wise, that is over $240,000 of additional salary for these women... and that's a conservative estimate with bonuses and such. When I think about aspirations for the future, I want these numbers to grow substantially.

I want thirteen women to earn promotions each week, or maybe even each day, with commensurate increases in compensation! Some people say they're not motivated by money, and I get that. But what the money can do is a motivator. Rachel is one of the thirteen women who received a promotion.

Since we've been working together in the 3 Pillars of Leadership course, Rachel has increased her salary by 52%. With that increase, she's been able to pay for travel volleyball for her daughter, put down a down payment on a car for her, and book a trip to Myrtle Beach for her daughter's Sweet 16 Birthday. She wouldn't have been able to do that without earning the promotions and increases in compensation.

I want more Sweet 16 trips, so to speak, for daughters of moms who are working and saying, "It sure is nice not to have to scrape for that money. I can just do this for her with ease."

The 3 Pillars of Leadership is my signature course. It complements the *Speak up, Sister!* book.

In the 3 Pillars of Leadership, the first pillar is strengthening self by building massive self-confidence. You can build confidence in the same way you do as a muscle. Results happen fast!

The second pillar is elevating communication. Once you've built strength of self in the first pillar, you're empowered to speak with an assertive voice and position yourself in front of the right people. Referring back to the story about how I got myself in front of Rich, I used some strategic communication techniques. I pass those, and more, along in the second pillar.

The third pillar is leveling up your career path. With an innate strength of self and elevated communication skills, it's time to level up your career path. Carrying yourself with executive presence and navigating higher-level conversations are two elements key to asking for, earning, and receiving a promotion.

It's the trifecta of strengthening self, elevating communication, and leveling up career path that is the winning combination for earning promotions, increasing compensation, and advancing careers.

We've all heard of the glass ceiling. It is at the top level, the C-suite. Along the way to the C-suite, however, there are stops at vice president, director, and senior manager.

The Broken Rung of the corporate ladder is notorious for preventing women from ascending the ladder. While companies are often equipped to advance women from entry-level to one rung above, the rungs often break after that. There is little to no guidance on how to advance a few years into one's career.

I figured out how to do it the hard way, though. I advanced my career three different times in three different male-dominated industries. I figured out a system. Today, that system is the 3 Pillars of Leadership. This is what I teach to other women motivated to advance their careers and more than capable of succeeding in next-level positions.

I want every woman to know this:

In a male-dominated industry, there is plenty of room for all of us. We don't need to elbow each other out of the way.

Cultivate your confidence, amplify your voice, and advance your career. The system to do it is there.

All you have to do is speak up and say you're ready!

closing impact statements

In the process of writing this book, we've challenged all the authors to put together a short sentence impact statement. It could be personal or professional, the choice was up to them.

Melissa Henault

The greatest impact one can have is through recognizing your God given gifts that positively impact the world, propagating a collective upward spiral on humanity. It is our most important quest in life... to hone in on our gifts and relentlessly perfect them for impact.

Julie Cober

I support ambitious professional women tapping into **AWARENESS** and **CLARITY,** giving them the leadership tools necessary to believe in themselves and design a business and life they love waking up to each and every day.

Darla Bonk

I consult entrepreneurs on how to build and live a life they love by falling back in love with their business and living life on purpose.

Annie Mirza

I empower accountants to build human-focused firms by creating beautiful websites that convert, innovative marketing strategies, and business coaching.

Genell Lemley

I guide and support high-performing women over 45 to prioritize and boost their brain health through transformative lifestyle changes, empowering them to live more energetic, vibrant, productive, and impactful lives.

Toni Burns

I customize and navigate through health benefit solutions for individuals, families, and small business owners, empowering them to secure health insurance solutions that serve their current needs and protect their future selves creating financial freedom.

Marissa Green

I use the power of connection and inspiration to help overworked moms step out of the hustle and into a life lived on their own terms.

Lisa Morris

I empower busy dynamic professional women to design, plan, and live their dream life from inception to all out through the success method.

Dr. Anjali Agrawal

I am a non-cracking, non-popping chiropractor who empowers families to navigate their health + wellness journey from conception to adulthood through structural alignment, functional nutrition, ergonomics, and unique diagnostic testing.

Ammie Michaels

I'm impacting the workplace through playful professional development and bridging the gap between human and artificial intelligence to empower teams and individuals with enhanced connection, communication, and collaboration.

Lauren Luedeke

I build strong foundations through honest and transparent email marketing.

Giselle Carson, Esq.

My team and I provide dynamic and responsive corporate immigration legal services, complemented by a holistic and innovative immigration academy tailored to C-suite, HR, and Legal leaders.

Claire Darr

I empower people to overcome burnout and stress through simple, proven systems so that they can embrace a vibrant and energetic life without sacrificing their careers or the success they've achieved.

Aimee Greczmiel

I help working mothers manage their mental and emotional wellness, so they may leave a lasting legacy for their family AND make an impact in their career.

Chelsea Larsen

Creating unforgettable family experiences through exceptional vacation rentals that foster, joy, connection, and lasting memories while helping vacation homeowners increase their rental income through providing white-glove property management services.

Jean Hansen

I work with entrepreneurs and parents of children with special needs to create a game plan for handling unexpected life events, providing them with confidence, reassurance, peace of mind, and allowing them to focus on life's joys instead of worrying about the unknown.

Stacia Hobson

I empower business leaders to go from "stuck" to making moves that pay.

Louise Taylor

I empower leaders to embrace vulnerability, ignite their inner light, and build authentic brands that resonate deeply and drive meaningful change.

Judy Tierney

I empower women to achieve financial independence through real estate investing and inspire them to create experiences for a more purposeful and rewarding life.

Carrie Peralta-Brummett

As a career coach, I help tech professionals unleash their potential to align their career journey with their desired life.

Tisha Castillo

I teach people to rethink food choices so they regain control over their health, reverse chronic conditions without relying on medications, and change their health trajectories—all in a way that is Simple AF.

Sara Davenport

As a journalist, I teach entrepreneurs the skills needed to share their stories so they can elevate their impact.

Jamie McKinney

I empower working women to amplify their voices, push fear aside, and earn promotions.

We want to challenge you, the reader, to put together your own impact statement. The purpose of this is to remind you of the difference you aim to make and to help you in your journey of achieving all-out impact.

_____

_____

_____

_____

full author conversations

Here you can find QR codes that link to author interviews with *all* the contributors in this book. *Yes, that's right, all of them!* Featured on the All Out Impact Podcast, each author has the opportunity to share additional background information, tips, and stories, addressing the 7 Big Questions.

These interviews offer a deeper dive into the context and answers to the 7 Big Questions. If you're looking for more advice, insight, or even a good laugh, enjoy the extended interviews listed by chapter order below.

Subscribe on Apple.　　　Subscribe on Spotify.　　　Follow on Audible.

Becoming The Ultimate Mentor
-MELISSA HENAULT

First, From Within
-JULIE COBER

Hope Dealer
-DARLA BONK

The Power of Intentional Impact
-ANNIE MIRZA

The Brain Health Revolution: Empowering Women to Take Charge of Their Brain Health
-GENELL LEMLEY

The Butterfly Effect
-TONI BURNS

The Power of a Village to Inspire an Authentic Transformation
- MARISSA GREEN

Cultivating a Legacy of Aligned Values
-LISA MORRIS

Move Well, Eat Well, Live Well
-DR. ANJALI AGRAWAL

Embracing Change: Empowering Teams
Through Emotional Intelligence and
Artificial Intelligence -AMMIE MICHAELS

The Impact of Community in Action
-LAUREN LUEDEKE

From Immigrant to Impact Maker
-GISELLE CARSON, ESQ.

Making the Most of Your Dash
-CLAIRE DARR

Reframing Pain & Embracing Change in
Motherhood
-AIMEE GRECZMIEL

From Heartache to Homecoming: Building
a Legacy of Family Memories
-CHELSEA LARSEN

The Value of Inclusive Connection
-JEAN HANSEN

Transforming a Male-Dominated Industry
through Female Leadership
-STACIA HOBSON

Unmasking Authenticity: Illuminating the
Path to Impactful Brands
-LOUISE TAYLOR

Beyond the Borders
-JUDY TIERNEY

You Are Empowered to Choose
-CARRIE PERALTA-BRUMMETT

From Heartache to Healing: A Mom's Mission to Rethink Food and Change Health Trajectories
-TISHA CASTILLO

The Impact of Storytelling
-SARA DAVENPORT

Rejection is Redirection
-JAMIE MCKINNEY

our favorite resources

Looking for *more* impactful resources? Here are some favorites from the authors, compiled specifically for you!

Free Business Planning Framework (focusing on impact and purpose),
BY MELISSA HENAULT

Oneness,
BY RASHA

The Untethered Soul,
BY MICHAEL SINGER

Tools of Titans,
BY TIM FERRISS

10% Happier,
BY DAN HARRIS

The Code of the Extraordinary Mind,
BY VISHEN LAKHIANI

On Our Best Behavior,
BY ELISE LOEHNEN

The Mel Robbins Podcast

Moms First "The Motherhood" Community

 Neha Ruche's "Mother Untitled" Community

 Ashley DelBello, Intuitive Life + Business Coach

 *Think and Grow Rich,*
BY NAPOLEON HILL

 *The One Thing,*
BY GARY KELLER AND JAY PAPASAN

top 7

IMPACT-DRIVEN BOTAO PODCAST EPISODES

Check out another resource that might encourage you along the way: The *Burnout To All Out Podcast*. This podcast covers lifestyle and business tips, along with tools to empower you to take the leap from burnout employees to all-out entrepreneurs. The best part? You can find these top 7 impact-driven episodes anywhere podcasts are available, making it easy for you to tune in from anywhere in the world!

EP. 44 | Finding Your Passion with Sandy and Wade Critides

EP. 110 | Making an Impact with Chris Harder

EP. 135 | Embrace Your Voice - It's Time to Tell Your Story

EP. 205 | Failure Teaches You the Most Important Business Lessons

EP. 216 | The Impact of Influencers on Your Business

EP. 217 | The Art of Making Connections

EP. 223 | How to Build a Connected Tribe

Find the most recent episodes at
burnouttoallout.co/podcast

create-your-own
actionable impact index
(AKA — A GUIDED IMPACT JOURNAL)

This index section provides blank lines for you to compile your own index based on the authors' chapters, quotes, and resources that resonate the most with you throughout this book. As you read, jot down some notes here to curate a personalized index.

> Ex: P.305 - Judy Tierney - "As an entrepreneur, integrating ethical and sustainable practices into my business is not just a choice, but a responsibility." ← This is SO true! As an entrepreneur it is my responsibility to...

This will serve as a quick and practical reference whenever you revisit this book. Think of this section as an impact journal. When you walk through wilderness seasons, open up this book, read through the conversations again, and continue writing notes to remind yourself of how YOU are uniquely called to make an All Out Impact!

Made in the USA
Middletown, DE
18 September 2024